Thank you...

...for purchasing this copy of Homework Today for ages 10-11. We hope that you will find these 50 photocopiable worksheets helpful as part of your programme for homework activities. Each sheet is accompanied by an answer sheet. If you wish to, you can photocopy the answer sheets as well to enable your pupils to check their own work. Some sheets, of course, include questions where the answers will be completed in an individual way by the pupils.

Please note that photocopies can only be made for use by the purchasing institution; supplying copies to other schools, institutions or individuals breaches the copyright licence. Thank you for your help in this.

Overleaf we have drafted a letter which you may wish to photocopy, or amend, to send home to parents.

This Homework Today book is part of our growing range of educational titles. Most of our books are individual workbooks but, due to popular demand, we are now introducing a greater number of photocopiable titles especially for teachers. You may like to look out for:

HOMEWORK TODAY for ages 7-8, 8-9, 9-10
WRITING FOR LITERACY for ages 5-7, 7-8, 8-9, 9-10, 10-11
SPELLING FOR LITERACY for ages 5-7, 7-8, 8-9, 9-10, 10-11
NUMERACY TODAY for ages 5-7, 7-9, 9-11
BEST HANDWRITING for ages 7-11

To find details of our other publications, please visit our website: **www.andrewbrodie.co.uk**

Dear Parents,

We are pleased to be providing homework sheets for our ten to eleven year old pupils, from a book called 'Homework Today'. These sheets contain activities which will enable your child to revise some of the skills and knowledge which they have acquired at school. The amount of time taken to complete each sheet will vary considerably but, as a guide, you should allow approximately 20 to 30 minutes per homework.

Try to help your child 'get into the homework habit' by providing a quiet place to work, with a desk or a table. Encourage your child to work in pen for written work and in pencil for maths. Neat presentation is important and reflects the pride your child takes in producing good quality work.

Thank you for supporting the work of the school by encouraging your child with homework.

Yours sincerely,

Homework Today is published by Andrew Brodie Publications.
Andrew Brodie Publications publish a range of educational workbooks for children,
available through bookstores or through the website: **www.andrewbrodie.co.uk**

Homework Today for ages 10 - 11 Contents Page

here are photocopiable record sheets inside the back cover.

Homework Today is published by Andrew Brodie Publications.
Andrew Brodie Publications publish a range of educational workbooks for children,
available through bookstores or through the website: **www.andrewbrodie.co.uk**

Name: Date:

Words and Numbers

Match the numbers to the words. The first one is done for you.

36 — two thousand, four hundred and ninety-three.
118   fourteen.
2493   thirty-six.
312   forty-two.
42   three hundred and twelve.
3249   one hundred and eighteen.
14   six hundred and four.
604   three thousand, two hundred and forty-nine.

Notice these spellings: four   fourteen   forty
                                                      Look: no 'u'

Use tidy handwriting to write these numbers in words:

614 ⟶

734 ⟶

2563 ⟶

9999 ⟶

7678 ⟶

Look at this
number:

Millions
Hundred thousands
Ten thousands
Thousands
Hundreds
Tens
Units

2 4 6 2 1 3 9

This number in words is…

…Two million, four hundred and
sixty-two thousand, one hundred
and thirty-nine.

Now match these numbers and words…

6507348   nineteen thousand, nine hundred and sixty-eight.
216573   six million, five hundred and seven thousand, three hundred and forty-eight.
4978056   four hundred and seventy-five thousand.
19968   two hundred and sixteen thousand, five hundred and seventy-three.
475000   eighty-two thousand.
82000   four million, nine hundred and seventy-eight thousand and fifty-six.

Write these numbers in words…

347192 ⟶

8208517 ⟶

© Andrew Brodie *Publications* ✓ PO Box 23, Wellington, Somerset, TA21 8YX ✓ www.andrewbrodie.co.uk

Words and Numbers

Match the numbers to the words. The first one is done for you.

36
118
2493
312
42
3249
14
604

two thousand, four hundred and ninety-three.
fourteen.
thirty-six.
forty-two.
three hundred and twelve.
one hundred and eighteen.
six hundred and four.
three thousand, two hundred and forty-nine.

Notice these spellings: four   fourteen   forty   Look: no 'u'

Use tidy handwriting to write these numbers in words:

614 ——→ six hundred and fourteen.

734 ——→ seven hundred and thirty-four.

2563 ——→ two thousand, five hundred and sixty-three.

9999 ——→ nine thousand, nine hundred and ninety-nine.

7678 ——→ seven thousand, six hundred and seventy-eight.

Look at this number:

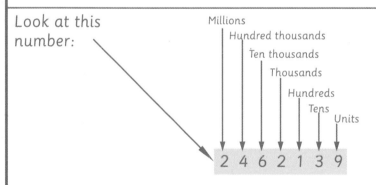

Millions
Hundred thousands
Ten thousands
Thousands
Hundreds
Tens
Units

2 4 6 2 1 3 9

This number in words is...
...Two million, four hundred and sixty-two thousand, one hundred and thirty-nine.

Now match these numbers and words...

6507348
216573
4978056
19968
475000
82000

nineteen thousand, nine hundred and sixty-eight.
six million, five hundred and seven thousand, three hundred and forty-eight.
four hundred and seventy-five thousand.
two hundred and sixteen thousand, five hundred and seventy-three.
eighty-two thousand.
four million, nine hundred and seventy-eight thousand and fifty-six.

Write these numbers in words...

347192 ——→ three hundred and forty-seven thousand, one hundred and ninety-two.

8208517 ——→ eight million, two hundred and eight thousand, five hundred and seventeen.

© Andrew Brodie *Publications* ✓ PO Box 23, Wellington, Somerset, TA21 8YX ✓ www.andrewbrodie.co.uk

Homework Today

Name: Date:

Multiplication Square

Time yourself...

Try to complete this multiplication square in less than eight minutes...

x	1	2	3	4	5	6	7	8	9	10
1										
2										
3										
4										
5										
6										
7										
8										
9										
10										

You can use the multiplication square to help answer division questions.

For example: We know that 63 ÷ 7 = 9
                because   7 x 9 = 63   and   9 x 7 = 63

Answer these sets of questions. Try to answer each set in less than 1 minute.

Set A	Set B	Set C	Set D
a 48 ÷ 6 =	**a** 8 ÷ 4 =	**a** 56 ÷ 8 =	**a** 4 ÷ 2 =
b 18 ÷ 3 =	**b** 24 ÷ 4 =	**b** 36 ÷ 6 =	**b** 49 ÷ 7 =
c 27 ÷ 9 =	**c** 36 ÷ 9 =	**c** 18 ÷ 2 =	**c** 25 ÷ 5 =
d 36 ÷ 4 =	**d** 72 ÷ 9 =	**d** 40 ÷ 5 =	**d** 36 ÷ 6 =
e 42 ÷ 7 =	**e** 12 ÷ 3 =	**e** 48 ÷ 8 =	**e** 64 ÷ 8 =
f 21 ÷ 7 =	**f** 28 ÷ 7 =	**f** 45 ÷ 9 =	**f** 16 ÷ 4 =
g 15 ÷ 3 =	**g** 42 ÷ 6 =	**g** 72 ÷ 8 =	**g** 81 ÷ 9 =
h 60 ÷ 10 =	**h** 54 ÷ 9 =	**h** 28 ÷ 4 =	**h** 9 ÷ 3 =

Name: Date:

Multiplication Square

Time yourself...
Try to complete this multiplication square in less than eight minutes...

x	1	2	3	4	5	6	7	8	9	10
1	1	2	3	4	5	6	7	8	9	10
2	2	4	6	8	10	12	14	16	18	20
3	3	6	9	12	15	18	21	24	27	30
4	4	8	12	16	20	24	28	32	36	40
5	5	10	15	20	25	30	35	40	45	50
6	6	12	18	24	30	36	42	48	54	60
7	7	14	21	28	35	42	49	56	63	70
8	8	16	24	32	40	48	56	64	72	80
9	9	18	27	36	45	54	63	72	81	90
10	10	20	30	40	50	60	70	80	90	100

You can use the multiplication square to help answer division questions.

For example: We know that $63 \div 7 = 9$
                because $7 \times 9 = 63$ and $9 \times 7 = 63$

Answer these sets of questions. Try to answer each set in less than 1 minute.

Set A	Set B	Set C	Set D
a 48 ÷ 6 = 8	**a** 8 ÷ 4 = 2	**a** 56 ÷ 8 = 7	**a** 4 ÷ 2 = 2
b 18 ÷ 3 = 6	**b** 24 ÷ 4 = 6	**b** 36 ÷ 6 = 6	**b** 49 ÷ 7 = 7
c 27 ÷ 9 = 3	**c** 36 ÷ 9 = 4	**c** 18 ÷ 2 = 9	**c** 25 ÷ 5 = 5
d 36 ÷ 4 = 9	**d** 72 ÷ 9 = 8	**d** 40 ÷ 5 = 8	**d** 36 ÷ 6 = 6
e 42 ÷ 7 = 6	**e** 12 ÷ 3 = 4	**e** 48 ÷ 8 = 6	**e** 64 ÷ 8 = 8
f 21 ÷ 7 = 3	**f** 28 ÷ 7 = 4	**f** 45 ÷ 9 = 5	**f** 16 ÷ 4 = 4
g 15 ÷ 3 = 5	**g** 42 ÷ 6 = 7	**g** 72 ÷ 8 = 9	**g** 81 ÷ 9 = 9
h 60 ÷ 10 = 6	**h** 54 ÷ 9 = 6	**h** 28 ÷ 4 = 7	**h** 9 ÷ 3 = 3

Name: Date:

Addition Grids

<u>Time yourself...</u>

Try to complete this addition square in less than eight minutes...

+	6	3	5	9	2	8	4	7	1
5									
7									
1									
4									
8									
6									
2									
3									
9									

Time yourself on each of these grids...

1

+	13	16	12	14
8				
6				
9				
7				

Time taken: [ ]

2

+	50	100	25	75
75				
100				
25				
50				

Time taken: [ ]

5

+	500	1000	1500
500			
1000			
1500			

Time taken: [ ]

4

+	250	500	750
250			
500			
750			

Time taken: [ ]

Answer Sheet

Number
3

Name: Date:

Addition Grids

Time yourself...
Try to complete this addition square in less than eight minutes...

+	6	3	5	9	2	8	4	7	1
5	11	8	10	14	7	13	9	12	6
7	13	10	12	16	9	15	11	14	8
1	7	4	6	10	3	9	5	8	2
4	10	7	9	13	6	12	8	11	5
8	14	11	13	17	10	16	12	15	9
6	12	9	11	15	8	14	10	13	7
2	8	5	7	11	4	10	6	9	3
3	9	6	8	12	5	11	7	10	4
9	15	12	14	18	11	17	13	16	10

Time yourself on each of these grids...

1

+	13	16	12	14
8	21	24	20	22
6	19	22	18	20
9	22	25	21	23
7	20	23	19	21

Time taken: [   ]

2

+	50	100	25	75
75	125	175	100	150
100	150	200	125	175
25	75	125	50	100
50	100	150	75	125

Time taken: [   ]

5

+	500	1000	1500
500	1000	1500	2000
1000	1500	2000	2500
1500	2000	2500	3000

Time taken: [   ]

4

+	250	500	750
250	500	750	1000
500	750	1000	1250
750	1000	1250	1500

Time taken: [   ]

© Andrew Brodie _Publications_ ✓ PO Box 23, Wellington, Somerset, TA21 8YX ✓ www.andrewbrodie.co.uk

Homework Today

Name: Date:

Finding Change

Change from 50p

50p – 26p =

50p – 38p =

50p – 19p =

50p – 47p =

50p – 13p =

50p – 8p =

50p – 29p =

50p – 11p =

50p – 32p =

50p – 21p =

Change from £1

£1 – 58p =

£1 – 25p =

£1 – 12p =

£1 – 46p =

£1 – 69p =

£1 – 75p =

£1 – 84p =

£1 – 57p =

£1 – 3p =

£1 – 61p =

Change from £5

£5 – £1·46 =

£5 – £3·93 =

£5 – £2·78 =

£5 – 7p =

£5 – £4·89 =

£5 – £3·53 =

£5 – £4·44 =

£5 – £1·95 =

£5 – £3·11 =

£5 – £2·06 =

Change from £10

£10 – £6·40 =

£10 – £2·97 =

£10 – £8·42 =

£10 – £5·01 =

£10 – £7·38 =

£10 – £9·23 =

£10 – £3·99 =

£10 – £1·16 =

£10 – 14p =

£10 – £4·85 =

£36

£32

Change from £100

How much change would I have from £100 if I bought...

... 1 table?

... 1 chair?

... 1 table and chair?

... 2 chairs?

... 1 table and 2 chairs?

Name: Date:

Finding Change

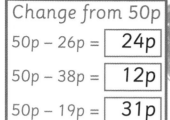

Change from 50p

50p – 26p =	24p
50p – 38p =	12p
50p – 19p =	31p
50p – 47p =	3p
50p – 13p =	37p
50p – 8p =	42p
50p – 29p =	21p
50p – 11p =	39p
50p – 32p =	18p
50p – 21p =	29p

Change from £1

£1 – 58p =	42p
£1 – 25p =	75p
£1 – 12p =	88p
£1 – 46p =	54p
£1 – 69p =	31p
£1 – 75p =	25p
£1 – 84p =	16p
£1 – 57p =	43p
£1 – 3p =	97p
£1 – 61p =	39p

Change from £5

£5 – £1·46 =	£3·54
£5 – £3·93 =	£1·07
£5 – £2·78 =	£2·22
£5 – 7p =	£4·93
£5 – £4·89 =	11p
£5 – £3·53 =	£1·47
£5 – £4·44 =	56p
£5 – £1·95 =	£3·05
£5 – £3·11 =	£1·89
£5 – £2·06 =	£2·94

Change from £10

£10 – £6·40 =	£3·60
£10 – £2·97 =	£7·03
£10 – £8·42 =	£1·58
£10 – £5·01 =	£4·99
£10 – £7·38 =	£2·62
£10 – £9·23 =	77p
£10 – £3·99 =	£6·01
£10 – £1·16 =	£8·84
£10 – 14p =	£9·86
£10 – £4·85 =	£5·15

£36

£32

Change from £100
How much change would I have from £100 if I bought…

… 1 table?	£64
… 1 chair?	£68
… 1 table and chair?	£32
… 2 chairs?	£36
… 1 table and 2 chairs?	none

Name: Date:

Measuring Angles

Angles which are less than a right-angle (90°) are called ACUTE angles.

Angles which are more than 90° but less than 180° are called OBTUSE angles.

Use a protractor to measure each of these angles. State whether each angle is acute or obtuse.

Example:

Acute

30°

1.

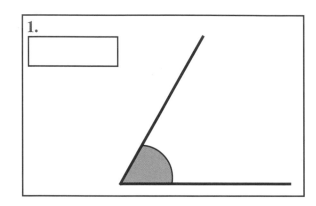

2.

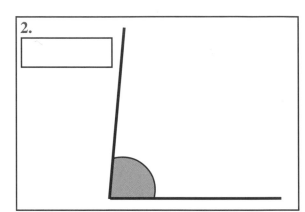

3.

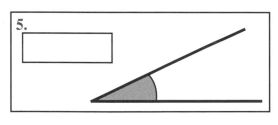

4.

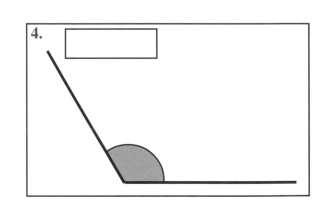

5.

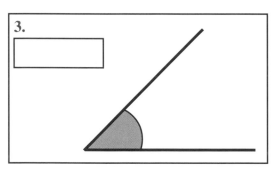

6.

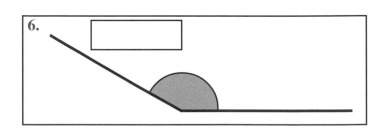

7.

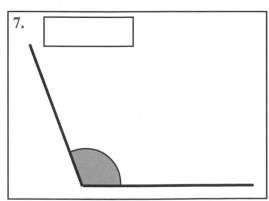

8.

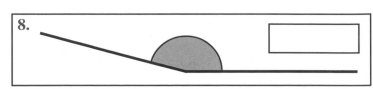

On the back of this sheet, draw some pairs of lines meeting at these angles:
85°, 72°, 115°, 28°, 16°, 152°

Name: Date:

Measuring Angles

Angles which are less than a right-angle (90°) are called ACUTE angles.

Angles which are more than 90° but less than 180° are called OBTUSE angles.

Use a protractor to measure each of these angles. State whether each angle is acute or obtuse.

Example:

Acute   30°

1.

acute

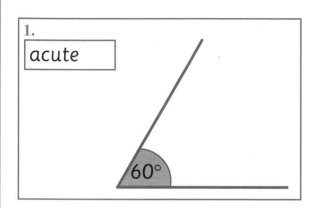

60°

2.

acute

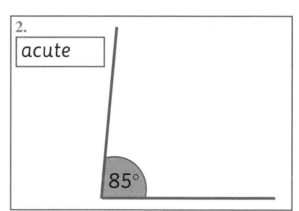

85°

3.

acute

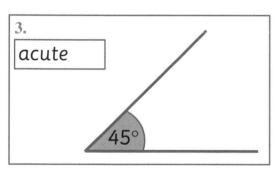

45°

4.

obtuse

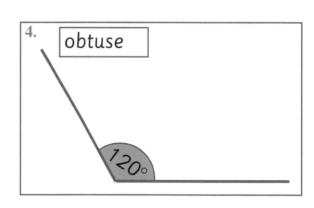

120°

5.

acute

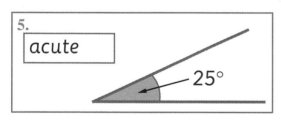

25°

6.

obtuse

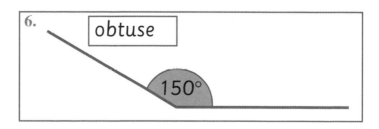

150°

7.

obtuse

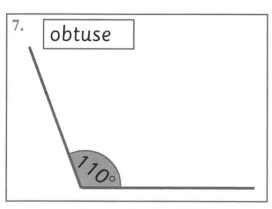

110°

8.

obtuse

165°

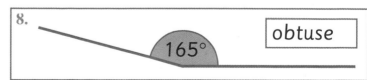

On the back of this sheet, draw some pairs of lines meeting at these angles:
85°, 72°, 115°, 28°, 16°, 152°

© Andrew Brodie *Publications* ✓ PO Box 23, Wellington, Somerset, TA21 8YX ✓ www.andrewbrodie.co.uk

Homework Today

Angles in a Triangle

The three angles in every triangle always add up to 180°.

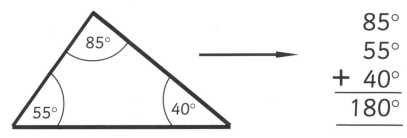

85°
55°
+ 40°
———
180°

If we know the sizes of two of the angles, we can work out the size of the other one...

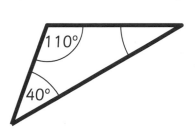

Step 1: Add the sizes of the two angles together:

110°
+ 40°
———
150°

Step 2: Subtract the answer from 180°:

180°
− 150°
———

This gives the size of the missing angle: ⟶ 30°

Find the missing angle sizes:

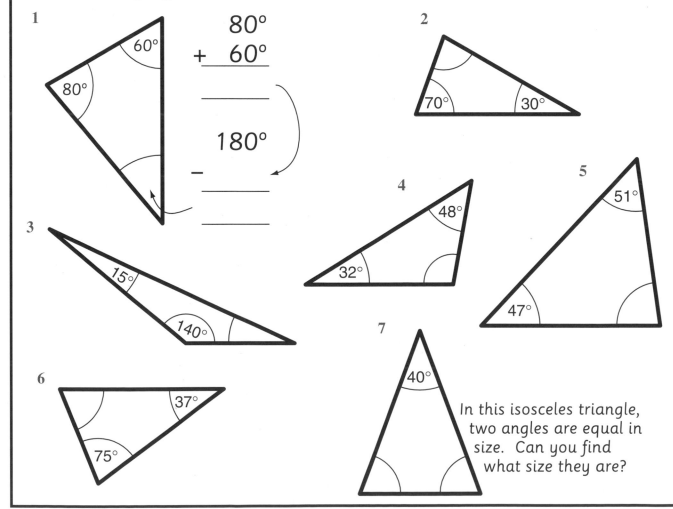

1

60°
80°

80°
+ 60°
———

180°
−
———
———

2

70°   30°

3

15°
140°

4

48°
32°

5

51°
47°

6

37°
75°

7

40°

In this isosceles triangle, two angles are equal in size. Can you find what size they are?

© Andrew Brodie *Publications* ✓ PO Box 23, Wellington, Somerset, TA21 8YX ✓ www.andrewbrodie.co.uk

Name: Date:

Angles in a Triangle

The three angles in
every triangle always
add up to 180°.

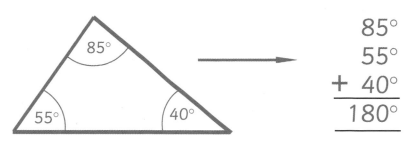

$$85°$$
$$55°$$
$$+\ 40°$$
$$\overline{180°}$$

If we know the sizes of two of the angles, we can work out the size of the other one...

Step 1:   Add the sizes of the
two angles together:

$$110°$$
$$+\ 40°$$
$$\overline{150°}$$

Step 2:   Subtract the answer
from 180°:

$$180°$$
$$-150°$$

This gives the size of the missing angle: $\longrightarrow$ $\underline{30°}$

Find the missing angle sizes:

1

$$80°$$
$$+\ 60°$$
$$\overline{140°}$$

$$180°$$
$$-140°$$
$$\overline{40°}$$

2

3

4

5

6

7

In this isosceles triangle,
two angles are equal in
size. Can you find
what size they are?

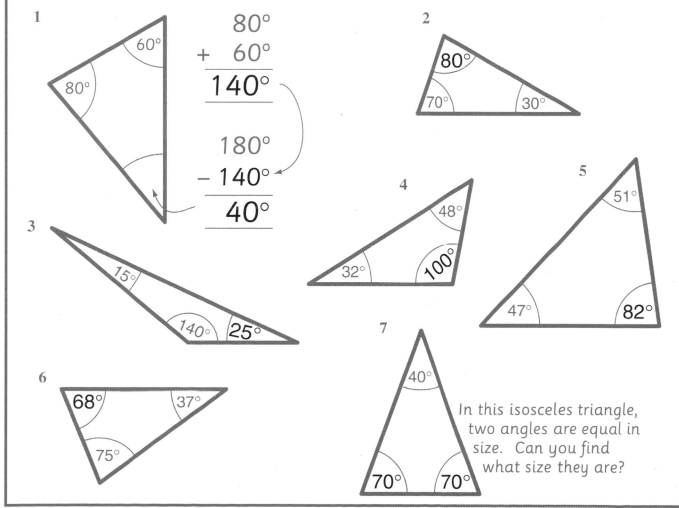

© Andrew Brodie *Publications* ✓ PO Box 23, Wellington, Somerset, TA21 8YX ✓ www.andrewbrodie.co.uk

Homework Today

Name: Date:

Magic Squares

In a magic square the numbers in every row, column and diagonal always add up to the same number.

Look carefully at this example:

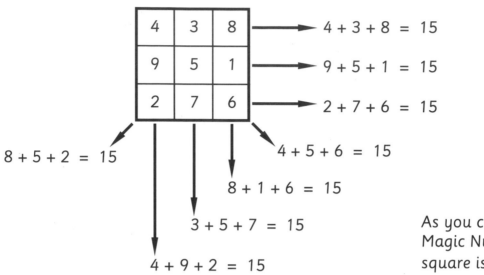

| 4 | 3 | 8 | → 4 + 3 + 8 = 15
| 9 | 5 | 1 | → 9 + 5 + 1 = 15
| 2 | 7 | 6 | → 2 + 7 + 6 = 15

8 + 5 + 2 = 15

4 + 5 + 6 = 15

8 + 1 + 6 = 15

3 + 5 + 7 = 15

4 + 9 + 2 = 15

As you can see, the Magic Number for this square is 15.

The magic squares below have some numbers missing. To find the missing numbers, follow these steps:

Step 1:   Find the Magic Number by adding a row, column or diagonal which has no missing numbers.

Step 2:   Look for a row, column or diagonal which has only one missing number.

Step 3:   Add the other numbers in the row, column or diagonal which you have chosen, then subtract this total from the Magic Number. You now have the number which will complete that line.

Step 4:   Keep working by always looking for a line with only one missing number.

Now try these:

		6
3	5	7

Magic number =

		8
11	9	7

Magic number =

		5
	6	
7		10

Magic number =

34	29	
		31
		33

Magic number =

Magic Squares

In a magic square the numbers in every row, column and diagonal always add up to the same number.

Look carefully at this example:

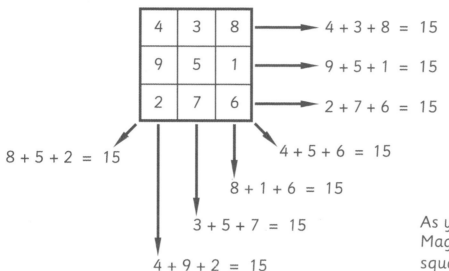

4 + 3 + 8 = 15

9 + 5 + 1 = 15

2 + 7 + 6 = 15

4 + 5 + 6 = 15

8 + 1 + 6 = 15

3 + 5 + 7 = 15

4 + 9 + 2 = 15

8 + 5 + 2 = 15

As you can see, the Magic Number for this square is 15.

The magic squares below have some numbers missing. To find the missing numbers, follow these steps:

<u>Step 1</u>:   Find the Magic Number by adding a row, column or diagonal which has no missing numbers.

<u>Step 2</u>:   Look for a row, column or diagonal which has only one missing number.

<u>Step 3</u>:   Add the other numbers in the row, column or diagonal which you have chosen, then subtract this total from the Magic Number. You now have the number which will complete that line.

<u>Step 4</u>:   Keep working by always looking for a line with only one missing number.

Now try these:

8	1	6
3	5	7
4	9	2

Magic number = 15

6	13	8
11	9	7
10	5	12

Magic number = 27

2	11	5
9	6	3
7	1	10

Magic number = 18

34	29	30
27	31	35
32	33	28

Magic number = 93

More Magic Squares

Try these 3 by 3 magic squares:

6		
11		
4		8

Magic number =

		17
		6
	14	16

Magic number =

6		
	8	
5		10

Magic number =

Now try these 4 by 4 magic squares:

	1		15
11	8	5	10
		9	
2			3

Magic number =

4	1		14
	10		
12	11		
	16	2	15

Magic number =

Can you complete this 5 by 5 magic square?

Remember:
Once you have found the Magic Number, always work on a line that has only one number missing.

10	27	20		6
9	13			
28	14	16	18	4
	21		19	25
26		12	15	

Magic number =

© Andrew Brodie *Publications* ✓ PO Box 23, Wellington, Somerset, TA21 8YX ✓ www.andrewbrodie.co.uk

Name: Date:

More Magic Squares

Try these 3 by 3 magic squares:

6	5	10
11	7	3
4	9	8

Magic number = 21

10	12	17
20	13	6
9	14	16

Magic number = 39

6	7	11
13	8	3
5	9	10

Magic number = 24

Now try these 4 by 4 magic squares:

14	1	4	15
11	8	5	10
7	12	9	6
2	13	16	3

Magic number = 34

4	1	19	14
17	10	8	3
12	11	9	6
5	16	2	15

Magic number = 38

Can you complete this 5 by 5 magic square?

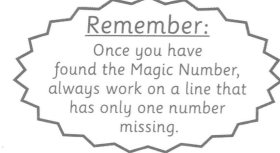

Remember:
Once you have
found the Magic Number,
always work on a line that
has only one number
missing.

10	27	20	17	6
9	13	24	11	23
28	14	16	18	4
7	21	8	19	25
26	5	12	15	22

Magic number = 80

Homework Today

Name: Date:

Area and Perimeter

Find the area and perimeter of each of the shapes shown. The first one is done for you.

1. Area = 1 cm²
    Perimeter = 4 cm

Remember:
...for area you should write each answer in square centimetres (cm²)
...for perimeter you should write each answer in centimetres (cm).

2. Area =
    Perimeter =

3. Area =
    Perimeter =

4. Area =
    Perimeter =

5. Area =
    Perimeter =

6. Area =
    Perimeter =

7. Area =   Perimeter =

8. Area =
    Perimeter =

9. Area =
    Perimeter =

10. Area =   Perimeter =

© Andrew Brodie *Publications* ✓ PO Box 23, Wellington, Somerset, TA21 8YX ✓ www.andrewbrodie.co.uk

Name: Date:

Area and Perimeter

Find the area and perimeter of each of the shapes shown. The first one is done for you.

1.
Area = 1 cm²
Perimeter = 4 cm

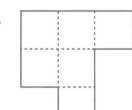

Remember:
…for area you should write each
answer in square centimetres (cm²)
…for perimeter you should write each
answer in centimetres (cm).

2.
Area = **3 cm²**
Perimeter = **8 cm**

3.
Area = **4 cm²**
Perimeter = **10 cm**

4.
Area = **5 cm²**
Perimeter = **10 cm**

5.
Area = **5 cm²**
Perimeter = **12 cm**

6.
Area = **6 cm²**
Perimeter = **12 cm**

7.
Area = **14 cm²**   Perimeter = **30 cm**

8.
Area = **7 cm²**
Perimeter = **12 cm**

9.
Area = **6 cm²**
Perimeter = **14 cm**

10.   Area = **24 cm²**   Perimeter = **28 cm**

Homework Today

Name: Date:

More Area and Perimeter

This rectangle is   4 cm long,
and 2 cm wide.

You can see that its area is 8 cm².
The area of a rectangle can be calculated by
multiplying its <u>length</u> by its <u>width</u>.

$$A = l \times w$$

The perimeter is found, of course, by adding the lengths of all the sides.

**Use your ruler to measure the length and width of each of the rectangles below.
Then calculate the area and perimeter of each one.**

1.
Length =
Width =
Area =
Perimeter =

2.
Length =
Width =
Area =
Perimeter =

3.
Length =
Width =
Area =
Perimeter =

4.
Length =   Area =
Width =   Perimeter =

5.
Length =
Width =
Area =
Perimeter =

6.
Length =   Area =
Width =   Perimeter =

7.
Length =
Width =
Area =
Perimeter =

© Andrew Brodie *Publications* ✓ PO Box 23, Wellington, Somerset, TA21 8YX ✓ www.andrewbrodie.co.uk

Name: Date:

More Area and Perimeter

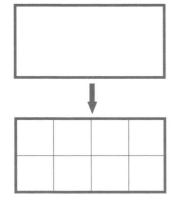

This rectangle is   4 cm long, and 2 cm wide.

You can see that its area is 8 cm². The area of a rectangle can be calculated by multiplying its <u>length</u> by its <u>width</u>.

$$A = l \times w$$

The perimeter is found, of course, by adding the lengths of all the sides.

Use your ruler to measure the length and width of each of the rectangles below. Then calculate the area and perimeter of each one.

1.

Length =   3 cm
Width =   2 cm
Area =   6 cm²
Perimeter = 10 cm

2.

Length =   5 cm
Width =   2 cm
Area = 10 cm²
Perimeter = 14 cm

3.

Length =   4 cm
Width =   2·5 cm
Area = 10 cm²
Perimeter = 13 cm

4.

Length = 6 cm   Area = 21 cm²
Width = 3·5 cm   Perimeter = 19 cm

5.

Length =   4·5 cm
Width =   2 cm
Area =   9 cm²
Perimeter = 13 cm

6.

Length = 5·5 cm   Area = 16·5 cm²
Width = 3 cm   Perimeter = 17 cm

7.

Length = 12 cm
Width =   1·5 cm
Area = 18 cm²
Perimeter = 27 cm

Name: Date:

Sequences

Look at this sequence of numbers:

| 6 | 10 | 14 | 18 | 22 | 26 | 30 | ... |

Now look at the pattern:

6 →+4→ 10 →+4→ 14 →+4→ 18 →+4→ 22 →+4→ 26 →+4→ 30 ...

...so the next number would be 34 and the one after would be 38 and so on.

For each of the sequences below, find the pattern then find the two missing numbers.
The pattern could be adding, subtracting, multiplying or dividing.

1.   2   4   6   8   10   12   ☐   ☐   ...

2.   50   45   40   35   30   25   ☐   ☐   ...

3. $\frac{1}{2}$ 1   2   4   8   16   ☐   ☐   ...

4.   96   48   24   12   6   ☐   ☐   ...

5.   25   50   75   100   125   150   175   ☐   ☐

6. Look carefully at the pattern in this one:

2   4   7   9   12   14   17   ☐   ☐

7. Here is another sequence with a complicated pattern:

8   12   11   15   14   18   17   ☐   ☐

On the back of this sheet, try creating 3 sequences of your own…

Name: _____   Date: _____

Sequences

Look at this sequence of numbers:

| 6 | 10 | 14 | 18 | 22 | 26 | 30 | ... |

Now look at the pattern:

6 →+4→ 10 →+4→ 14 →+4→ 18 →+4→ 22 →+4→ 26 →+4→ 30 ...

...so the next number would be 34 and the one after would be 38 and so on.

For each of the sequences below, find the pattern then find the two missing numbers.
The pattern could be adding, subtracting, multiplying or dividing.

1. 2 →+2→ 4 →+2→ 6 →+2→ 8 →+2→ 10 →+2→ 12 →+2→ [14] →+2→ [16] ...

2. 50 →−5→ 45 →−5→ 40 →−5→ 35 →−5→ 30 →−5→ 25 →−5→ [20] →−5→ [15] ...

3. $\frac{1}{2}$ →x2→ 1 →x2→ 2 →x2→ 4 →x2→ 8 →x2→ 16 →x2→ [32] →x2→ [64] ...

4. 96 →÷2→ 48 →÷2→ 24 →÷2→ 12 →÷2→ 6 →÷2→ [3] →÷2→ [1·5] ...

5. 25 →+25→ 50 →+25→ 75 →+25→ 100 →+25→ 125 →+25→ 150 →+25→ 175 →+25→ [200] →+25→ [225]

6. Look carefully at the pattern in this one:

2 →+2→ 4 →+3→ 7 →+2→ 9 →+3→ 12 →+2→ 14 →+3→ 17 →+2→ [19] →+3→ [22]

7. Here is another sequence with a complicated pattern:

8 →+4→ 12 →−1→ 11 →+4→ 15 →−1→ 14 →+4→ 18 →−1→ 17 →+4→ [21] →−1→ [20]

On the back of this sheet, try creating 3 sequences of your own...

© Andrew Brodie *Publications* ✓ PO Box 23, Wellington, Somerset, TA21 8YX ✓ www.andrewbrodie.co.uk

Homework Today

Name: Date:

Adding Decimals

Adding decimals is easy:
     ✔ keep the units in the correct columns
     ✔ keep the decimal points in line

Look at these examples...

$4·2 + 3·6$

$$\begin{array}{r} 4·2 \\ +\underline{3·6} \\ \underline{7·8} \end{array}$$

$16 + 2·9$

$$\begin{array}{r} 16·0 \\ +\underline{2·9} \\ \underline{18·9} \end{array}$$

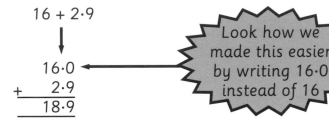

Look how we made this easier by writing 16·0 instead of 16

Answer these questions by setting out the sums correctly:

1. $2·7 + 1·2$

2. $5·3 + 2·4$

3. $12·6 + 4·1$

4. $18·7 + 5·9$

Try these:

5. $6·9 + 4$

6. $13 + 6·8$

7. $17 + 9·9$

8. $48·3 + 69$

Now try these:

9. $12·2 + 1·65$

10. $16 + 4·8 + 3·91$

11. $25·4 + 13 + 6·58$

Answer these questions on a separate piece of paper:

12. $26·8 + 13·9$

13. $84·23 + 16·97$

14. $126 + 87·4 + 19·98$

Name: Date:

Adding Decimals

Adding decimals is easy:
- ✔ keep the units in the correct columns
- ✔ keep the decimal points in line

Look at these examples...

$4 \cdot 2 + 3 \cdot 6$

$$\begin{array}{r} 4 \cdot 2 \\ +\ \ 3 \cdot 6 \\ \hline 7 \cdot 8 \end{array}$$

$16 + 2 \cdot 9$

$$\begin{array}{r} 16 \cdot 0 \\ +\ \ 2 \cdot 9 \\ \hline 18 \cdot 9 \end{array}$$

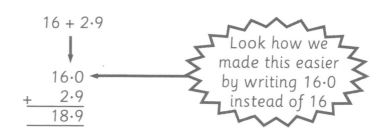

Look how we made this easier by writing 16·0 instead of 16

Answer these questions by setting out the sums correctly:

1. $2 \cdot 7 + 1 \cdot 2$

$$\begin{array}{r} 2 \cdot 7 \\ +\ \ 1 \cdot 2 \\ \hline 3 \cdot 9 \end{array}$$

2. $5 \cdot 3 + 2 \cdot 4$

$$\begin{array}{r} 5 \cdot 3 \\ +\ \ 2 \cdot 4 \\ \hline 7 \cdot 7 \end{array}$$

3. $12 \cdot 6 + 4 \cdot 1$

$$\begin{array}{r} 12 \cdot 6 \\ +\ \ 4 \cdot 1 \\ \hline 16 \cdot 7 \end{array}$$

4. $18 \cdot 7 + 5 \cdot 9$

$$\begin{array}{r} 18 \cdot 7 \\ +\ \ 5 \cdot 9 \\ \hline 24 \cdot 6 \end{array}$$

Try these:

5. $6 \cdot 9 + 4$

$$\begin{array}{r} 6 \cdot 9 \\ +\ \ 4 \cdot 0 \\ \hline 10 \cdot 9 \end{array}$$

6. $13 + 6 \cdot 8$

$$\begin{array}{r} 13 \cdot 0 \\ +\ \ 6 \cdot 8 \\ \hline 19 \cdot 8 \end{array}$$

7. $17 + 9 \cdot 9$

$$\begin{array}{r} 17 \cdot 0 \\ +\ \ 9 \cdot 9 \\ \hline 26 \cdot 9 \end{array}$$

8. $48 \cdot 3 + 69$

$$\begin{array}{r} 48 \cdot 3 \\ +\ \ 69 \cdot 0 \\ \hline 117 \cdot 3 \end{array}$$

Now try these:

9. $12 \cdot 2 + 1 \cdot 65$

$$\begin{array}{r} 12 \cdot 20 \\ +\ \ 1 \cdot 65 \\ \hline 13 \cdot 85 \end{array}$$

10. $16 + 4 \cdot 8 + 3 \cdot 91$

$$\begin{array}{r} 16 \cdot 00 \\ 4 \cdot 80 \\ +\ \ 3 \cdot 91 \\ \hline 24 \cdot 71 \end{array}$$

11. $25 \cdot 4 + 13 + 6 \cdot 58$

$$\begin{array}{r} 25 \cdot 40 \\ 13 \cdot 00 \\ +\ \ 6 \cdot 58 \\ \hline 44 \cdot 98 \end{array}$$

Answer these questions on a separate piece of paper:

12. $26 \cdot 8 + 13 \cdot 9 = 40 \cdot 7$

13. $84 \cdot 23 + 16 \cdot 97 = 101 \cdot 2$

14. $126 + 87 \cdot 4 + 19 \cdot 98 = 233 \cdot 38$

Name: Date:

Coordinates

Four points are marked on the grid.

    Point A has coordinates (2, 1)

    Point B has coordinates (,)

    Point C has coordinates (,)

    Point D has coordinates (,)

Using a pencil and a ruler draw lines to join A to B, B to C, C to D and D to A.
What shape have you drawn?

Now draw the diagonals of the shape by joining A to C and B to D.

What are the coordinates of the point where they cross? (,)

Using a different colour, mark these coordinates on the grid: (3, 4) (9, 4) (6, 12).

Now join the points. What type of triangle have you made?

Choose another colour then mark on these coordinates:
    (8, 3) (6, 6) (10, 9) (12, 7) (11, 2)
Join the points together. Notice that this shape is not regular.

How many sides has it got?   What shape is it?

© Andrew Brodie *Publications* ✓ PO Box 23, Wellington, Somerset, TA21 8YX ✓ www.andrewbrodie.co.uk

Name: Date:

Coordinates

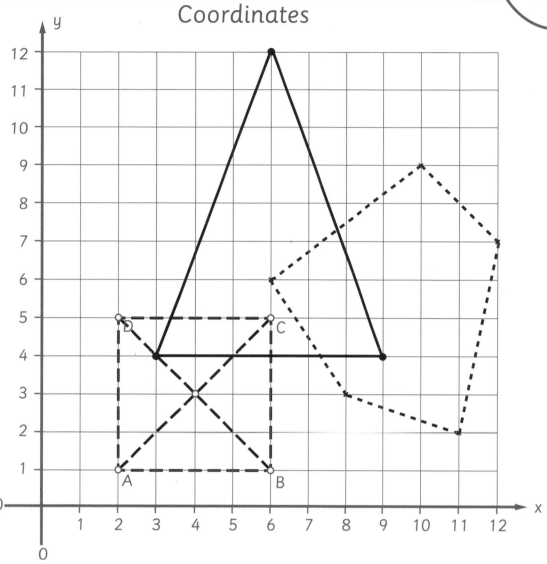

Four points are marked on the grid.

Point A has coordinates (2, 1)

Point B has coordinates (6 , 1)

Point C has coordinates (6 , 5)

Point D has coordinates (2 , 5)

Using a pencil and a ruler draw lines to join A to B, B to C, C to D and D to A.
What shape have you drawn?

square

Now draw the diagonals of the shape by joining A to C and B to D.

What are the coordinates of the point where they cross? (4 , 3)

Using a different colour, mark these coordinates on the grid: (3, 4) (9, 4) (6, 12).

Now join the points. What type of triangle have you made?   isosceles

Choose another colour then mark on these coordinates:
   (8, 3) (6, 6) (10, 9) (12, 7) (11, 2)

Join the points together. Notice that this shape is not regular.

How many sides has it got?   5   What shape is it?   pentagon

© Andrew Brodie *Publications* ✓ PO Box 23, Wellington, Somerset, TA21 8YX ✓ www.andrewbrodie.co.uk

Name: Date:

Handling Data 1

Jim and Sarah measured the temperature outside the school buildings every Monday, Wednesday and Friday over four weeks. They plotted the results on a graph:

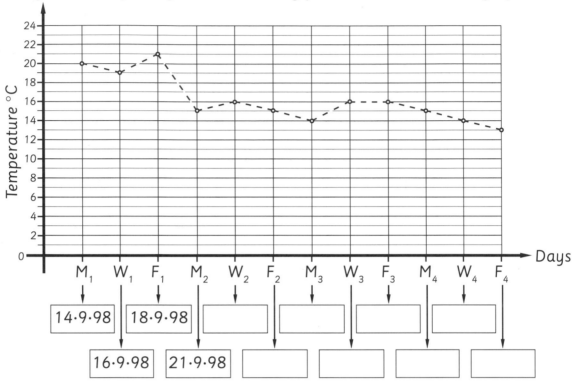

14·9·98   18·9·98

16·9·98   21·9·98

Mark in the dates in the boxes provided. The first few are done for you.

1.   On what date was the first Wednesday (W_1)?

2.   On what date was the second Friday (F_2)?

3.   On what date was the third Wednesday (W_3)?

4.   What day of the week was 1st October?

5. (a) What is the highest temperature recorded on the graph?

            (b) On what date was this?

6. (a) What is the lowest temperature recorded on the graph?

            (b) On what date was this?

7.   What is the difference between the highest

        and the lowest temperatures recorded?

8.   On what dates were temperatures of 16°C recorded?

© Andrew Brodie *Publications* ✓ PO Box 23, Wellington, Somerset, TA21 8YX ✓ www.andrewbrodie.co.uk

Name: Date:

Handling Data 1

Jim and Sarah measured the temperature outside the school buildings every Monday, Wednesday and Friday over four weeks. They plotted the results on a graph:

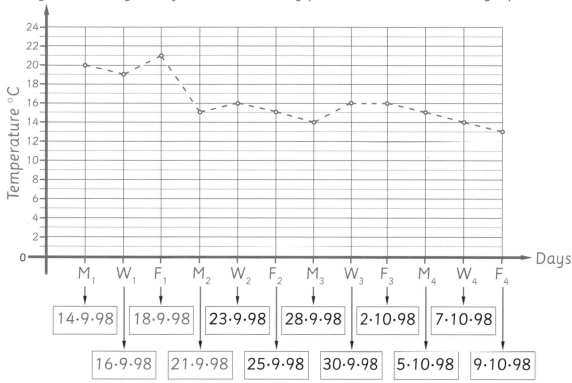

Mark in the dates in the boxes provided. The first few are done for you.

1.   On what date was the first Wednesday (W_1)?   16·9·98

2.   On what date was the second Friday (F_2)?   25·9·98

3.   On what date was the third Wednesday (W_3)?   30·9·98

4.   What day of the week was 1st October?   Thursday

5. (a) What is the highest temperature recorded on the graph? 21°C

           (b) On what date was this?   18·9·98

6. (a) What is the lowest temperature recorded on the graph? 13°C

           (b) On what date was this?   9·10·98

7.   What is the difference between the highest

      and the lowest temperatures recorded?   8°C

8.   On what dates were temperatures of 16°C recorded?

      23·9·98   30·9·98   2·10·98

© Andrew Brodie *Publications* ✓ PO Box 23, Wellington, Somerset, TA21 8YX ✓ www.andrewbrodie.co.uk

Handling Data 2

Temperature data was collected every day for a week, starting on a Sunday.
A graph was made.

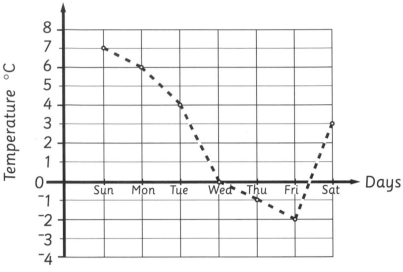

Use the graph to enter data in the table below.
Two temperatures have already been entered for you.

Sunday	Monday	Tuesday	Wednesday	Thursday	Friday	Saturday
			0°C		⁻2°C	

From the graph we can see that...

    ...the greatest drop in temperature was between Tuesday and Wednesday

        when the temperature fell by ☐.

    ...the greatest rise in temperature was between ☐ and ☐

        when the temperature rose by ☐.

    ...the warmest day was ☐.

    ...the coldest day was ☐.

    ...the temperature range was ☐.

On which three days would there have been ice on puddles?

☐ ☐ ☐

In what season of the year were the temperatures recorded? ☐

How much warmer was Monday than Thursday? ☐

How much cooler was Friday than Saturday? ☐

Name: Date:

Handling Data 2

Temperature data was collected every day for a week, starting on a Sunday.
A graph was made.

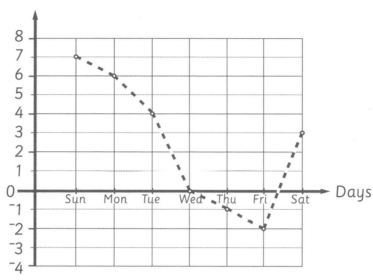

Use the graph to enter data in the table below.
Two temperatures have already been entered for you.

Sunday	Monday	Tuesday	Wednesday	Thursday	Friday	Saturday
7°C	6°C	4°C	0°C	⁻1°C	⁻2°C	3°C

From the graph we can see that...

...the greatest drop in temperature was between Tuesday and Wednesday

when the temperature fell by ‖ 4°C ‖.

...the greatest rise in temperature was between ‖ Friday ‖ and ‖ Saturday ‖

when the temperature rose by ‖ 5°C ‖.

...the warmest day was ‖ Sunday ‖.

...the coldest day was ‖ Friday ‖.

...the temperature range was ‖ 9°C ‖.

On which three days would there have been ice on puddles?

‖ Wednesday ‖   ‖ Thursday ‖   ‖ Friday ‖

In what season of the year were the temperatures recorded? ‖ Winter ‖

How much warmer was Monday than Thursday? ‖ 7°C ‖

How much cooler was Friday than Saturday? ‖ 5°C ‖

Name: Date:

Handling Data 3

Temperatures were recorded every day for 9 days in June.
The data is shown in this table.

1st June	2nd June	3rd June	4th June	5th June	6th June	7th June	8th June	9th June
18°C	21°C	21°C	21°C	20°C	22°C	23°C	23°C	20°C

Which temperature represents the mode? ☐

What is the median temperature? ☐

What is the temperature range? ☐

What is the mean temperature? ☐

Complete the graph below by…
    …labelling the axes,
    …entering the data from the table above,
    …writing an appropriate title,
    …joining the points with lines.

The median is found by putting the data in order from smallest to largest and finding the middle number.

The mean is found by adding all the data together, then dividing by the number of entries.

The mode is the number which occurs most often in the list.

The range is the highest piece of data minus the lowest.

Name: Date:

Handling Data 3

Temperatures were recorded every day for 9 days in June.
The data is shown in this table.

1st June	2nd June	3rd June	4th June	5th June	6th June	7th June	8th June	9th June
18°C	21°C	21°C	21°C	20°C	22°C	23°C	23°C	20°C

Which temperature represents the mode? 21°C

What is the median temperature? 21°C

What is the temperature range? 5°C

What is the mean temperature? 21°C

The median is found by putting the data in order from smallest to largest and finding the middle number.

Complete the graph below by…
  …labelling the axes,
  …entering the data from the table above,
  …writing an appropriate title,
  …joining the points with lines.

The mean is found by adding all the data together, then dividing by the number of entries.

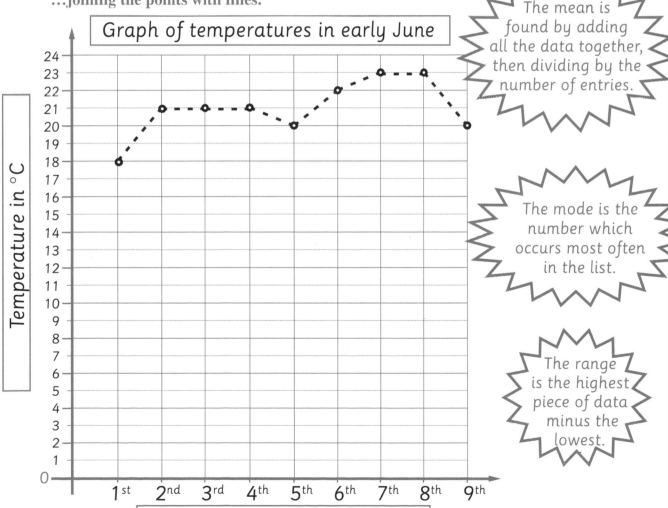

Graph of temperatures in early June

Temperature in °C

Dates in June

The mode is the number which occurs most often in the list.

The range is the highest piece of data minus the lowest.

© Andrew Brodie *Publications* ✓ PO Box 23, Wellington, Somerset, TA21 8YX ✓ www.andrewbrodie.co.uk

Homework Today

Name: Date:

The Moon

Read this passage then answer the questions which follow it.

Like the Sun and the Earth, the Moon is spherical in shape. The Earth takes one year to travel around the Sun. The Moon accompanies the Earth on its journey around the Sun, all the time making its own journey around the Earth. The Moon travels completely around the Earth approximately every twenty-eight days. As the Moon orbits the Earth, it spins slowly on its own axis, again taking approximately twenty-eight days to do so.

The first person to step on to the Moon was Neil Armstrong, an American astronaut. This took place in 1969. Eleven other astronauts visited the Moon over a period of three years. Before travelling to the Moon all of them had to be trained to deal with the low gravity they would find there. The gravity of the Moon is approximately one-sixth the gravity of the Earth.

Use the information above to help you in answering the questions below.

1. Draw a ring around the correct statement:

The Moon travels around the Earth...

> ...twenty-eight times per year.

> ...once per year.

> ...every night.

> ...once every twenty-eight days.

2. What shape is the Moon? _____

3. Who was the first person to set foot on the Moon? _____

4. Altogether, how many people have walked on the Moon? _____

5. In which year did people last walk on the Moon? _____

6. How many years ago is that? _____

or the Internet/www

Use an encyclopedia to find two other facts about the Moon.
Write your facts on the back of this sheet.

© Andrew Brodie *Publications* ✓ PO Box 23, Wellington, Somerset, TA21 8YX ✓ www.andrewbrodie.co.uk

Name: Date:

The Moon

Read this passage then answer the questions which follow it.

Like the Sun and the Earth, the Moon is spherical in shape. The Earth takes one year to travel around the Sun. The Moon accompanies the Earth on its journey around the Sun, all the time making its own journey around the Earth. The Moon travels completely around the Earth approximately every twenty-eight days. As the Moon orbits the Earth, it spins slowly on its own axis, again taking approximately twenty-eight days to do so.

The first person to step on to the Moon was Neil Armstrong, an American astronaut. This took place in 1969. Eleven other astronauts visited the Moon over a period of three years. Before travelling to the Moon all of them had to be trained to deal with the low gravity they would find there. The gravity of the Moon is approximately one-sixth the gravity of the Earth.

Use the information above to help you in answering the questions below.

1. Draw a ring around the correct statement:

   The Moon travels around the Earth...

   | ...twenty-eight times per year. | ...once per year. | ...every night. | ...once every twenty-eight days. |

   (...once every twenty-eight days. is circled)

2. What shape is the Moon? __A sphere__

3. Who was the first person to set foot on the Moon? __Neil Armstrong__

4. Altogether, how many people have walked on the Moon? __12__

5. In which year did people last walk on the Moon? __1972__

6. How many years ago is that? _____
   This answer depends on the date of the current year.
   Use an encyclopedia to find two other facts about the Moon.
   Write your facts on the back of this sheet.

Balloon Flight

An early morning mist still hung between the trees in the valley and the grass all around us was soaked with the dampness of autumn. The pilot instructed us to unroll the material along the ground. Ian and I did as we were told and unrolled the bulky canvas into a long ribbon shape. We then had to pull the material out to the sides, revealing the balloon's colours. We had been expecting them to be bright but they consisted of red and a dull blue and both colours had faded over time.

Once connected to the wicker basket, which was lying on its side, the canopy was inflated, first with a high-power fan and then with the giant gas burners themselves. The basket was pulled upright, then the four of us, including the pilot and another passenger, climbed in. There was only just enough space for the four of us to stand around the bottle of gas.

Moments later, the burners provided enough lift for the balloon to start to rise. The gentle breeze carried us across the field, then we felt the warm blast of the burners and rose rapidly to clear the tall trees at the field's edge.

Draw a ring around the answer to this question:

What does this second sentence tell us?
   The pilot instructed us to unroll the material along the ground.

that the pilot was bossy	that the passengers helped to prepare the balloon	that the pilot was too lazy to do the job himself	that the material was damp

Put the following sentences in the correct order by numbering each one.
The first one is done for you.

[ ] The basket was pulled upright.

[1] The material was unrolled along the ground.

[ ] The canopy was inflated, firstly with a fan.

[ ] The balloon rose rapidly.

[ ] Four people climbed into the balloon.

On the back of the sheet, write your own description of the balloon,
using the information contained in the passage.

© Andrew Brodie *Publications* ✓ PO Box 23, Wellington, Somerset, TA21 8YX ✓ www.andrewbrodie.co.uk

Name: Date:

Balloon Flight

An early morning mist still hung between the trees in the valley and the grass all around us was soaked with the dampness of autumn. The pilot instructed us to unroll the material along the ground. Ian and I did as we were told and unrolled the bulky canvas into a long ribbon shape. We then had to pull the material out to the sides, revealing the balloon's colours. We had been expecting them to be bright but they consisted of red and a dull blue and both colours had faded over time.

Once connected to the wicker basket, which was lying on its side, the canopy was inflated, first with a high-power fan and then with the giant gas burners themselves. The basket was pulled upright, then the four of us, including the pilot and another passenger, climbed in. There was only just enough space for the four of us to stand around the bottle of gas.

Moments later, the burners provided enough lift for the balloon to start to rise. The gentle breeze carried us across the field, then we felt the warm blast of the burners and rose rapidly to clear the tall trees at the field's edge.

Draw a ring around the answer to this question:

What does this second sentence tell us?
    The pilot instructed us to unroll the material along the ground.

that the pilot was bossy	that the passengers helped to prepare the balloon	that the pilot was too lazy to do the job himself	that the material was damp

Put the following sentences in the correct order by numbering each one.
The first one is done for you.

3	The basket was pulled upright.
1	The material was unrolled along the ground.
2	The canopy was inflated, firstly with a fan.
5	The balloon rose rapidly.
4	Four people climbed into the balloon.

On the back of the sheet, write your own description of the balloon,
using the information contained in the passage.

© Andrew Brodie *Publications* ✓ PO Box 23, Wellington, Somerset, TA21 8YX ✓ www.andrewbrodie.co.uk

Homework Today

Name: _____ Date: _____

Verbs

Draw a ring around the verbs in the sentences below.
Be careful because there may be more than one verb in a sentence.

The fat cat is chasing a thin mouse.

Sidney ran to the bus stop.

The owl swooped down and grabbed a beetle.

The verbs have been missed out of the sentences below.
For each sentence choose the verb which will make the most sense, from the list provided.

We _____ down the road very quickly.

cried   swam   walked   talked   sailed

The dentist _____ my teeth with his mirror.

examined   drilled   polished   cleaned   extracted

I _____ the grape pips by mistake.

planted   watered   swallowed   flattened   squeezed

Find suitable verbs to fill the gaps in this passage:

Yesterday we _____ up to High Moor. The bus _____ us at Beam

Bridge, from where we _____ our expedition. We _____ alongside the

stream which, in some places, _____ through narrow gaps in the rocks.

Eventually we _____ to _____ over the stream so that we could

_____ up the other side. We couldn't _____ a place where it was easy to

_____ but we did _____ a spot where there was a boulder in the middle

of the stream. We _____ onto the boulder then, from there, _____ to the

other side. Most of us _____ over safely but Sam _____ into the water.

She was absolutely soaked.

Name: _____ Date: _____

Verbs

Draw a ring around the verbs in the sentences below.
Be careful because there may be more than one verb in a sentence.

The fat cat is (chasing) a thin mouse.

Sidney (ran) to the bus stop.

The owl (swooped) down and (grabbed) a beetle.

The verbs have been missed out of the sentences below.
For each sentence choose the verb which will make the most sense, from the list provided.

We __walked__ down the road very quickly.

cried   swam   walked   talked   sailed

The dentist __examined__ my teeth with his mirror.

examined   drilled   polished   cleaned   extracted

I __swallowed__ the grape pips by mistake.

planted   watered   swallowed   flattened   squeezed

Find suitable verbs to fill the gaps in this passage:
You may have found better words than the ones shown here...

Yesterday we __walked__ up to High Moor. The bus __dropped__ us at Beam Bridge, from where we __started__ our expedition. We __walked__ alongside the stream which, in some places, __rushed__ through narrow gaps in the rocks. Eventually we __tried__ to __cross__ over the stream so that we could __walk__ up the other side. We couldn't __find__ a place where it was easy to __cross__ but we did __find__ a spot where there was a boulder in the middle of the stream. We __jumped__ onto the boulder then, from there, __leaped__ to the other side. Most of us __crossed__ over safely but Sam __fell__ into the water. She was absolutely soaked.

© Andrew Brodie *Publications* ✓ PO Box 23, Wellington, Somerset, TA21 8YX ✓ www.andrewbrodie.co.uk

Nouns and Pronouns

Underline the <u>common nouns</u> in these sentences:

The dog ran along the street.   (2 common nouns)

Pete's car suddenly began rolling down the hill.   (2 common nouns)

We ran over the bridge, down the stairs and
on to the platform just as the train pulled out
of the station.   (5 common nouns)

Underline the <u>proper nouns</u> in the sentences below.
Remember that proper nouns always start with a capital letter.

On Monday, Jasdeep went to Ealing.

Next March, Jan will be eleven years old.

During the months of April, May and June, Steve
     walked from Land's End to John O'Groats.

Look at these two sentences:

Jack picked some strawberries.
Jack ate the strawberries with some cream.

In the second sentence we have repeated the proper noun, Jack, and the common noun,
strawberries. It would be better if we replaced these two nouns with <u>pronouns:</u>

Jack picked some strawberries. <u>He</u> ate <u>them</u> with some cream.

Write a second sentence for each of the sentences below. Use pronouns where you can.

Holly carried the bags of shopping to the car.

‒ ‒

In the summer, David plays cricket.

‒ ‒

Uncle Ian and Aunty Sue showed Dan and Rob their new boat.

‒ ‒

‒ ‒

© Andrew Brodie *Publications* ✓ PO Box 23, Wellington, Somerset, TA21 8YX ✓ www.andrewbrodie.co.uk

Name: Date:

Nouns and Pronouns

Underline the <u>common nouns</u> in these sentences:

The <u>dog</u> ran along the <u>street.</u>   (2 common nouns)

Pete's <u>car</u> suddenly began rolling down the <u>hill.</u>   (2 common nouns)

We ran over the <u>bridge,</u> down the <u>stairs</u> and
on to the <u>platform</u> just as the <u>train</u> pulled out
of the <u>station.</u>   (5 common nouns)

Underline the <u>proper nouns</u> in the sentences below.
Remember that proper nouns always start with a capital letter.

On <u>Monday,</u> <u>Jasdeep</u> went to <u>Ealing.</u>

Next <u>March,</u> <u>Jan</u> will be eleven years old.

During the months of <u>April,</u> <u>May</u> and <u>June,</u> <u>Steve</u>
walked from <u>Land's End</u> to <u>John O'Groats.</u>

Look at these two sentences:

Jack picked some strawberries.
Jack ate the strawberries with some cream.

In the second sentence we have repeated the proper noun, Jack, and the common noun,
strawberries. It would be better if we replaced these two nouns with <u>pronouns:</u>

Jack picked some strawberries. <u>He</u> ate <u>them</u> with some cream.

Write a second sentence for each of the sentences below. Use pronouns where you can.
        The answers to this section will be created by the individual pupil.
Holly carried the bags of shopping to the car.

_ _

In the summer, David plays cricket.

_ _

Uncle Ian and Aunty Sue showed Dan and Rob their new boat.

_ _
_ _

© Andrew Brodie *Publications* ✓ PO Box 23, Wellington, Somerset, TA21 8YX ✓ www.andrewbrodie.co.uk

Adjectives

Yesterday was a marvellous day. We went swimming at the new pool then we had a gorgeous pizza for lunch.

Max

In talking about what happened yesterday, Max used three describing words (adjectives):
marvellous, new and gorgeous

Underline the adjectives in this sentence:
Happy Harry drove his shiny, new blue car into the wide garage of his big house.

Write suitable adjectives in the gaps provided:

The soup is _____ .

I went to see a _____ film.

I tried to pat the _____ _____ dog.

Write a short account of something which happened today. Use as many adjectives as you can, if they are appropriate.

_____

_____

_____

_____

Comparative adjectives

Sometimes we wish to compare things.
        For example: This mountain is high.
                                That mountain is higher but the one in the distance is highest.
The adjectives high, higher and highest are used to compare the three mountains.

Complete this chart of comparative adjectives:

big	bigger	....
happy	happier	....
good	....	....

small	....	smallest
....	....	softest
bad	....	....

Sometimes, to make comparisons we need to use the words more or most:
        This flower is beautiful.
                        That one is .... beautiful.
                                The red one is the .... beautiful.

© Andrew Brodie *Publications* ✓ PO Box 23, Wellington, Somerset, TA21 8YX ✓ www.andrewbrodie.co.uk

Name: Date:

Adjectives

> Yesterday was a marvellous day. We went swimming at the new pool then we had a gorgeous pizza for lunch.

Max

In talking about what happened yesterday, Max used three describing words (adjectives):
marvellous, new and gorgeous

Underline the adjectives in this sentence:
<u>Happy</u> Harry drove his <u>shiny</u>, <u>new</u> <u>blue</u> car into the <u>wide</u> garage of his <u>big</u> house.

Write suitable adjectives in the gaps provided:

The soup is _____ .

I went to see a _____ film.

I tried to pat the _____ _____ dog.

Answers to be selected by individual pupils.

Write a short account of something which happened today. Use as many adjectives as you can, if they are appropriate.

The response to this will be created by individual pupils.

_____

_____

_____

_____

Comparative adjectives

Sometimes we wish to compare things.
    For example: This mountain is high.
                    That mountain is higher but the one in the distance is highest.
The adjectives high, higher and highest are used to compare the three mountains.

Complete this chart of comparative adjectives:

big	bigger	biggest
happy	happier	happiest
good	better	best

small	smaller	smallest
soft	softer	softest
bad	worse	worst

Sometimes, to make comparisons we need to use the words more or most:
    This flower is beautiful.
                    That one is more beautiful.
                    The red one is the most beautiful.

Name: Date:

Adverbs

The dog barked loudly.

In this sentence the verb is <u>barked.</u>
The word <u>loudly</u> tells us <u>how</u> the dog barked. This type of word is called an adverb.
Underline the adverbs in these sentences:

We watched the teacher writing neatly on the board.

The rain fell heavily as we waited quietly.

Sam did his maths carefully.

Choose suitable adverbs to fill the gaps:

The red car was travelling very _____ .

She dived _____ into the pool.

Eliza whispered _____ so that only I could hear her.

Write two sentences about something you have done today. Try to use suitable adverbs.

_____

_____

_____

Comparative Adverbs

Look at this sentence:

Max is working <u>more carefully</u> than Minnie.

We sometimes use the word <u>more</u> when we are comparing how something is being done.
Rewrite the <u>sentences below</u>. Select from…

(more carefully)   (louder)   (more kindly)   (faster)

I could not have been treated …

_____

Lucy completed the work .... than anyone else.

_____

Dave swam the length of the pool .... than all the others.

_____

_____

My dog was barking .... than all the others at the dog show.

_____

_____

Name: Date:

Adverbs

The dog barked loudly.

In this sentence the verb is <u>barked</u>.

The word <u>loudly</u> tells us <u>how</u> the dog barked. This type of word is called an adverb.

Underline the adverbs in these sentences:

We watched the teacher writing <u>neatly</u> on the board.

The rain fell <u>heavily</u> as we waited <u>quietly.</u>

Sam did his maths <u>carefully.</u>

Choose suitable adverbs to fill the gaps:

The red car was travelling very _____ .

She dived _____ into the pool.

Eliza whispered _____ so that only I could hear her.

Answers to be selected by individual pupils.

Write two sentences about something you have done today. Try to use suitable adverbs.

_____

Pupils choose their own responses.

_____

_____

Comparative Adverbs

Look at this sentence:

Max is working <u>more carefully</u> than Minnie.

We sometimes use the word <u>more</u> when we are comparing how something is being done.

Rewrite the <u>sentences below</u>. Select from…

(more carefully) (louder)   (more kindly)   (faster)

I could not have been treated …

<u>I could not have been treated more kindly.</u>

Lucy completed the work .... than anyone else.

<u>Lucy completed the work more carefully than anyone else.</u>

Dave swam the length of the pool .... than all the others.

<u>Dave swam the length of the pool faster than all the others.</u>

My dog was barking .... than all the others at the dog show.

<u>My dog was barking louder than all the others at the show.</u>

© Andrew Brodie *Publications* ✓ PO Box 23, Wellington, Somerset, TA21 8YX ✓ www.andrewbrodie.co.uk

Singular and Plural

Fill the gaps in this chart:

Singular	Plural
horse	horses
match	
	women
boy	
	girls
tooth	
	wolves
sheep	
	feet

Look at this sentence:

The boy is eating his dinner with a spoon.

If there were two boys instead of one, look how the sentence would be:

The boys <u>are</u> eating <u>their</u> dinner<u>s</u> with spoon<u>s</u>.

In each sentence below, the subject of the sentence is singular. Rewrite each one, making the subject plural. Make sure that you change all the words you need to.

The tree is bending in the wind.

_ _

The man was riding his bike.

_ _

When a baby is asleep its mother gets some peace.

_ _

This newspaper is too big.

_ _

If the dog barks, please let him out.

_ _

That tree needs to be cut down.

_ _

The calf has eaten all the grass.

_ _

© Andrew Brodie *Publications* ✓ PO Box 23, Wellington, Somerset, TA21 8YX ✓ www.andrewbrodie.co.uk

Name: _____   Date: _____

Singular and Plural

Fill the gaps in this chart:

Singular	Plural
horse	horses
match	**matches**
woman	women
boy	**boys**
girl	girls
tooth	**teeth**
wolf	wolves
sheep	**sheep**
foot	feet

Look at this sentence:

The boy is eating his dinner with a spoon.

If there were two boys instead of one, look how the sentence would be:

The boys <u>are</u> eating <u>their</u> dinner<u>s</u> with spoon<u>s</u>.

In each sentence below, the subject of the sentence is singular. Rewrite each one, making the subject plural. Make sure that you change all the words you need to.

The tree is bending in the wind.

The trees are bending in the wind. _____

The man was riding his bike.

The men were riding their bikes. _____

When a baby is asleep its mother gets some peace.

When babies are asleep their mothers get some peace. _____

This newspaper is too big.

These newspapers are too big. _____

If the dog barks, please let him out.

If the dogs bark, please let them out. _____

That tree needs to be cut down.

Those trees need to be cut down. _____

The calf has eaten all the grass.

The calves have eaten all the grass. _____

© Andrew Brodie *Publications* ✓ PO Box 23, Wellington, Somerset, TA21 8YX ✓ www.andrewbrodie.co.uk

Using Apostrophes 1

When we speak, we often run two words together.
For example, we say "don't" instead of "do not".

do not ⟶ don't

the apostrophe has been put in to replace the letter "o" in "not".

will not ⟶ won't

we change this word completely when we say "won't".

Rewrite the sentences below. Where you can, run two words together and use an apostrophe to replace the missing letters.

It is a lovely day today.

_ _

She is going to buy a pop magazine.

_ _

We are working on fractions at school and I do not like them.

_ _

_ _

When I am older I am going to live in the city.

_ _

_ _

I can not finish my homework until later.

_ _

_ _

Read a page from your reading book. Write the name of the book and the page that you are reading on the back of this sheet.
Write down any words you find which have been shortened using apostrophes.

Using Apostrophes 1

When we speak, we often run two words together.
For example, we say "don't" instead of "do not".

do not ⟶ don't

the apostrophe has been put in to replace the letter "o" in "not".

will not ⟶ won't

we change this word completely when we say "won't".

Rewrite the sentences below. Where you can, run two words together and use an apostrophe to replace the missing letters.

It is a lovely day today.

It's a lovely day today. _ _ _ _ _ _ _ _ _ _ _ _ _ _ _ _ _

She is going to buy a pop magazine.

She's going to buy a pop magazine. _ _ _ _ _ _ _ _ _ _ _

We are working on fractions at school and I do not like them.

We're working on fractions at school and I don't like them.

_ _

When I am older I am going to live in the city.

When I'm older I'm going to live in the city. _ _ _ _ _ _

_ _

I can not finish my homework until later.

I can't finish my homework until later. _ _ _ _ _ _ _ _ _

_ _

Read a page from your reading book. Write the name of the book and the page that you are reading on the back of this sheet.
Write down any words you find which have been shortened using apostrophes.

© Andrew Brodie *Publications* ✓ PO Box 23, Wellington, Somerset, TA21 8YX ✓ www.andrewbrodie.co.uk

Name: Date:

Using Apostrophes 2

Apostrophes can be used to show ownership or possession.

The apostrophe is used to show that the shirt belongs to Tom.

Tom's shirt has got paint on it.

Rewrite these sentences, putting in the missing apostrophes.

I went to Marys house yesterday.

_____

The birds foot was caught in the cage door.

_____

Jacks cat chased Sarahs dog into Mr. Browns garden.

_____

_____

The girls ran to collect Daves shoes.

_____

(Notice that, in this sentence, the girls do not own anything so the word <u>girls</u> does not have an apostrophe.)

Dad collected Marks bike and took it to Tims house where
Mark was staying for the night.

_____

_____

Now write a sentence of your own in which you use an apostrophe to show ownership..

_____

_____

Read a page from your reading book. Write the name of the book and the page number on the back of this sheet. If you find any words where apostrophes have been used to show ownership, write them down.

© Andrew Brodie *Publications* ✓ PO Box 23, Wellington, Somerset, TA21 8YX ✓ www.andrewbrodie.co.uk

Name: Date:

Using Apostrophes 2

Apostrophes can be used to show ownership or possession.

The apostrophe is used to show that the shirt belongs to Tom.

Tom's shirt has got paint on it.

Rewrite these sentences, putting in the missing apostrophes.

I went to Marys house yesterday.

I went to Mary's house yesterday. _ _ _ _ _ _ _ _ _ _ _ _ _ _ _

The birds foot was caught in the cage door.

The bird's foot was caught in the cage door. _ _ _ _ _ _ _ _ _ _ _

Jacks cat chased Sarahs dog into Mr. Browns garden.

Jack's cat chased Sarah's dog into Mr. Brown's garden. _ _ _ _ _

_ _

The girls ran to collect Daves shoes.

The girls ran to collect Dave's shoes. _ _ _ _ _ _ _ _ _ _ _ _ _ _

(Notice that, in this sentence, the girls do not own anything so the word <u>girls</u> does not have an apostrophe.)

Dad collected Marks bike and took it to Tims house where Mark was staying for the night.

Dad collected Mark's bike and took it to Tim's house where Mark

was staying for the night. _ _ _ _ _ _ _ _ _ _ _ _ _ _ _ _ _ _

Now write a sentence of your own in which you use an apostrophe to show ownership..

Pupil to create own sentence. _ _ _ _ _ _ _ _ _ _ _ _ _ _ _ _ _ _

_ _

Read a page from your reading book. Write the name of the book and the page number on the back of this sheet. If you find any words where apostrophes have been used to show ownership, write them down.

© Andrew Brodie *Publications* ✓ PO Box 23, Wellington, Somerset, TA21 8YX ✓ www.andrewbrodie.co.uk

Using Apostrophes 3

When something is owned by more than one person we often have to put an apostrophe after the letter s instead of before it.

Look: This is the boy's house. This is the boys' house.

The first sentence shows us that there is only one boy. The second sentence shows us that more than one boy lives in this house. (Remember: the word "boy" is singular, the word "boys" is plural.)

Rewrite the sentences below, putting in the missing apostrophes. You will need to decide whether there is one owner or more than one owner in each case.

That girls hair is in her eyes.

_ _

The girls changing rooms are on the right and
the boys changing rooms are on the left.

_ _

_ _

As you know, some plural words do not have a letter 's' on the end. For example, the plural of child is children.

Look at the apostrophes in these two sentences:

The child's coat is on her peg.
The other children's coats are all over the floor.

In the first sentence, the coat belongs to one child. In the second sentence the coats belong to several children.

Rewrite these sentences putting in the missing apostrophes and remembering to check who things belong to.

The womens clothes are expensive in this shop.

_ _

The cats blanket is on the chair.

_ _

The five dogs leads were hanging in a row.

_ _

Using Apostrophes 3

When something is owned by more than one person we often have to put an apostrophe after the letter s instead of before it.

Look: This is the boy's house.   This is the boys' house.

The first sentence shows us that there is only one boy. The second sentence shows us that more than one boy lives in this house. (Remember: the word "boy" is singular, the word "boys" is plural.)

Rewrite the sentences below, putting in the missing apostrophes. You will need to decide whether there is one owner or more than one owner in each case.

That girls hair is in her eyes.

_ _ That girl's hair is in her eyes. _ _ _ _ _ _ _ _ _ _ _ _ _ _ _ _ _

The girls changing rooms are on the right and
the boys changing rooms are on the left.

_ _ The girls' changing rooms are on the right and the boys' _ _ _

_ _ changing rooms are on the left. _ _ _ _ _ _ _ _ _ _ _ _ _ _ _

As you know, some plural words do not have a letter 's' on the end. For example, the plural of child is children.

Look at the apostrophes in these two sentences:

    The child's coat is on her peg.
    The other children's coats are all over the floor.

In the first sentence, the coat belongs to one child. In the second sentence the coats belong to several children.

Rewrite these sentences putting in the missing apostrophes and remembering to check who things belong to.

The womens clothes are expensive in this shop.

_ _ The women's clothes are expensive in this shop. _ _ _ _ _ _ _

The cats blanket is on the chair.

_ _ The cat's blanket is on the chair. _ _ _ _ _ _ _ _ _ _ _ _ _ _

The five dogs leads were hanging in a row.

_ _ The five dogs' leads were hanging in a row. _ _ _ _ _ _ _ _ _ _

© Andrew Brodie *Publications* ✓ PO Box 23, Wellington, Somerset, TA21 8YX ✓ www.andrewbrodie.co.uk

Punctuation Practice 1

Rewrite each of these sentences correctly.
Be careful because they become more difficult as you go down the page.

we walked to the shop to buy some milk

_____

the journey to london was very boring

_____

i have a good friend called sam

_____

she went to her friends house on thursday

_____

the boys coats were all over the cloakroom floor

_____

my uncle tony bought a television a video and a camcorder
when he went to singapore.

_____

_____

new york washington chicago los angeles and dallas are all
cities in the united states of america

_____

_____

_____

© Andrew Brodie *Publications* ✓ PO Box 23, Wellington, Somerset, TA21 8YX ✓ www.andrewbrodie.co.uk

Punctuation Practice 1

Rewrite each of these sentences correctly.
Be careful because they become more difficult as you go down the page.

we walked to the shop to buy some milk

We walked to the shop to buy some milk.

the journey to london was very boring

The journey to London was very boring.

i have a good friend called sam

I have a good friend called Sam.

she went to her friends house on thursday

She went to her friend's house on Thursday.

the boys coats were all over the cloakroom floor

The boys' coats were all over the cloakroom floor.

my uncle tony bought a television a video and a camcorder
when he went to singapore.

My Uncle Tony bought a television, a video and a camcorder
when he went to Singapore.

new york washington chicago los angeles and dallas are all
cities in the united states of america

New York, Washington, Chicago, Los Angeles and Dallas are
all cities in the United States of America.

Name: Date:

Punctuation Practice 2

All the punctuation has been left out of this passage:

a slight breeze blew in through the open window each time it did so the curtains fluttered open and the early morning sunlight sneaked into the room with it eliza didnt notice at first but slept on dreaming of bright flashes from cameras at last however the bright flashes of sunlight and the gentle breeze were enough to stir her she opened her eyes then put her hand over them as the sun burst in again eliza its time to get up her mother called eliza lifted her pillow from under her head and placed it over it instead perfect she thought i cant see the sunlight and i cant hear mum

Rewrite the passage putting in punctuation. Remember that some people may punctuate it slightly differently from others. The important thing is to make sure it makes sense.

_____

_____

_____

_____

_____

_____

_____

_____

_____

_____

_____

_____

_____

_____

_____

_____

_____

_____

© Andrew Brodie *Publications* ✓ PO Box 23, Wellington, Somerset, TA21 8YX ✓ www.andrewbrodie.co.uk

Punctuation Practice 2

All the punctuation has been left out of this passage:

a slight breeze blew in through the open window each time it did so the curtains fluttered open and the early morning sunlight sneaked into the room with it eliza didnt notice at first but slept on dreaming of bright flashes from cameras at last however the bright flashes of sunlight and the gentle breeze were enough to stir her she opened her eyes then put her hand over them as the sun burst in again eliza its time to get up her mother called eliza lifted her pillow from under her head and placed it over it instead perfect she thought i cant see the sunlight and i cant hear mum

Rewrite the passage putting in punctuation. Remember that some people may punctuate it slightly differently from others. The important thing is to make sure it makes sense.

A slight breeze blew in through the open window. Each time it did so the curtains fluttered open and the early morning sunlight sneaked into the room with it. Eliza didn't notice at first but slept on, dreaming of bright flashes from cameras. At last, however, the bright flashes of sunlight and the gentle breeze were enough to stir her. She opened her eyes, then put her hand over them as the sun burst in again.

"Eliza, it's time to get up," her mother called.

Eliza lifted her pillow from under her head and placed it over it instead. 'Perfect,' she thought. 'I can't see the sunlight and I can't hear Mum.'

© Andrew Brodie *Publications* ✓ PO Box 23, Wellington, Somerset, TA21 8YX ✓ www.andrewbrodie.co.uk

Punctuation Practice 3

Look at this short conversation:

"Do you want to play football?" asked Dave.
"Yes," replied Tristan.
"Shall we see if Alan wants to come?"
"Could do."

There are some important things to notice:

    1. **When a person speaks, a new line is started.**

    2. **The second set of speech marks always has another punctuation mark with it.**
       Look:

       ?"   ,"   ."

    3. **The second set of speech marks always comes <u>after</u> the other punctuation mark.**

       For example, this is correct: ?" ✔

       These are wrong: "? ✘   "? ✘

The conversation below is unpunctuated. Rewrite it using appropriate punctuation.

whats on at the cinema asked hannah theres nothing i want to see said tom shall we go bowling instead then hannah asked that would be good replied tom

_____

_____

_____

_____

_____

_____

Now make up a conversation between two people and write the conversation out:

_____

_____

_____

_____

_____

© Andrew Brodie *Publications* ✓ PO Box 23, Wellington, Somerset, TA21 8YX ✓ www.andrewbrodie.co.uk

Name: Date:

Punctuation Practice 3

Look at this short conversation:

> "Do you want to play football?" asked Dave.
> "Yes," replied Tristan.
> "Shall we see if Alan wants to come?"
> "Could do."

There are some important things to notice:

1. **When a person speaks, a new line is started.**
2. **The second set of speech marks always has another punctuation mark with it.**
   Look:

3. **The second set of speech marks always comes <u>after</u> the other punctuation mark.**

For example, this is correct: ✔

These are wrong: ✘   ✘

The conversation below is unpunctuated. Rewrite it using appropriate punctuation.

whats on at the cinema asked hannah theres nothing i want to see said tom shall we go bowling instead then hannah asked that would be good replied tom

---

"What's on at the cinema?" asked Hannah.

"There's nothing I want to see," said Tom.

"Shall we go bowling instead then?" Hannah asked.

"That would be good," replied Tom.

Now make up a conversation between two people and write the conversation out:

_____

_____

_____

_____

Name: Date:

Titanic

The Titanic set sail from Southampton at noon on Wednesday 10th April 1912. This was to be the ship's maiden voyage to New York, stopping first at Cherbourg in France then at Queenstown, Ireland, to pick up extra passengers.

The Titanic and her sister ship the Olympic, were bigger than any transatlantic liners that had been built before them. Titanic was approximately two hundred and sixty-eight metres long. She had four funnels and, measured from the very top of the funnels to the keel at the bottom of the ship, she had a height of approximately fifty-three metres.

At about twenty minutes before midnight on Sunday 14th April, Titanic struck an iceberg which tore a hole in the side of the ship. Water flooded in and the slow process of sinking began. Over the next few hours, many people fell or jumped into the freezing cold sea. They were not among the lucky ones who managed to find places on the ship's lifeboats. Nobody is totally sure how many people were travelling on the Titanic, though there were probably about two thousand, two hundred and twenty passengers and crew altogether. Of these, approximately seven hundred and five survived.

Draw a ring around each correct answer:

Titanic set sail on 10th April 1912 from:

New York   Cherbourg   Southampton   Queenstown

The length of the Titanic was approximately:

fifty-three metres   two hundred and sixty-eight metres

The bottom of the ship is called the:

keel   bow   funnel   stern

Answer the following questions:

At what time of day did Titanic set sail?

Where did Titanic stop on the voyage?

At what time of day did Titanic hit the iceberg?

Approximately how many people did not survive the disaster?

Use an encyclopedia to find two more facts about the Titanic.
Write them on the back of this sheet.

© Andrew Brodie *Publications* ✓ PO Box 23, Wellington, Somerset, TA21 8YX ✓ www.andrewbrodie.co.uk

Titanic

The Titanic set sail from Southampton at noon on Wednesday 10ᵗʰ April 1912. This was to be the ship's maiden voyage to New York, stopping first at Cherbourg in France then at Queenstown, Ireland, to pick up extra passengers.

The Titanic and her sister ship the Olympic, were bigger than any transatlantic liners that had been built before them. Titanic was approximately two hundred and sixty-eight metres long. She had four funnels and, measured from the very top of the funnels to the keel at the bottom of the ship, she had a height of approximately fifty-three metres.

At about twenty minutes before midnight on Sunday 14ᵗʰ April, Titanic struck an iceberg which tore a hole in the side of the ship. Water flooded in and the slow process of sinking began. Over the next few hours, many people fell or jumped into the freezing cold sea. They were not among the lucky ones who managed to find places on the ship's lifeboats. Nobody is totally sure how many people were travelling on the Titanic, though there were probably about two thousand, two hundred and twenty passengers and crew altogether. Of these, approximately seven hundred and five survived.

Draw a ring around each correct answer:

Titanic set sail on 10ᵗʰ April 1912 from:

New York   Cherbourg   ⬭Southampton⬭   Queenstown

The length of the Titanic was approximately:

fifty-three metres   ⬭two hundred and sixty-eight metres⬭

The bottom of the ship is called the:

⬭keel⬭   bow   funnel   stern

Answer the following questions:

At what time of day did Titanic set sail? noon

Where did Titanic stop on the voyage? Cherbourg   Queenstown

At what time of day did Titanic hit the iceberg? 11·40pm

Approximately how many people did not survive the disaster? 1515

Use an encyclopedia to find two more facts about the Titanic.
Write them on the back of this sheet.

© Andrew Brodie *Publications* ✓ PO Box 23, Wellington, Somerset, TA21 8YX ✓ www.andrewbrodie.co.uk

Homework Today

Name: Date:

Pairs of words

Find the opposites of the following words...

up	....	open	....	big	....
near	....	lift	....	kind	....
heavy	....	under	....	happiness	....
dark	....	wide	....	in	....

Give the past tense of the verbs given:

(e.g. I <u>ride</u> my bike   ⟶   I <u>rode</u> my bike)

ride	....	dig	....	buy	....
sing	....	live	....	give	....
go	....	think	....	bring	....
shout	....	scratch	....	hit	....

Look at these pairs of words:

grass, green : snow, ...

The best word to fit the gap is 'white'.

Try to find the best words to fit the gaps in these pairs:

dog, kennel : rabbit, ...

sky, birds : sea, ...

day, sun : night, ...

feet, toes : hands, ...

carrot, vegetable : apple, ...

feet, socks : hands, ...

patients, hospital : pupils, ...

chair, furniture : spoon, ...

roof, tiles : ...., bricks.

bread, eat : water, ...

Name: Date:

Pairs of words

Find the opposites of the following words...

up	...down	open	...close.	big	...small...........
near	...far.....	lift	...drop.	kind	...unkind.........
heavy	...light.	under	...over..	happiness	...sadness........
dark	...light.	wide	...narrow	in	...out..............

Please note: alternative correct answers may be selected by pupils.

Give the past tense of the verbs given:

(e.g. I <u>ride</u> my bike ⟶ I <u>rode</u> my bike)

ride	..rode..	dig	..dug......	buy	..bought...
sing	..sang..	live	..lived.....	give	..gave........
go	..went.	think	..thought	bring	..brought..
shout	..shouted	scratch	..scratched	hit	..hit...........

Look at these pairs of words:

grass, green : snow, ...

The best word to fit the gap is 'white'.

Try to find the best words to fit the gaps in these pairs:

dog, kennel : rabbit, ...hutch... .

sky, birds : sea, ...fish...... .

day, sun : night, ...moon or stars

feet, toes : hands, ...fingers.. .

carrot, vegetable : apple, ...fruit..... .

feet, socks : hands, ...gloves.. .

patients, hospital : pupils, ...school... .

chair, furniture : spoon, ...cutlery.. .

roof, tiles : ...wall....., bricks.

bread, eat : water, ...drink... .

© Andrew Brodie *Publications* ✓ PO Box 23, Wellington, Somerset, TA21 8YX ✓ www.andrewbrodie.co.uk

Morse Code

In 1837, an American named Samuel Morse invented a system of sending messages through wires. This system was called the telegraph and was operated by sending electrical impulses along wires. The message had to be sent by using a special code, called Morse Code.

In Morse Code, letters are represented by dots and dashes. You can send Morse Code messages yourself by using a torch - quick flashes make the dots and longer flashes make the dashes. The most famous Morse Code signal is S.O.S., used by ships in distress.

Here is the Morse Code alphabet:

A · –	B – · · ·	C – · – ·	D – · ·	E ·	F · · – ·
G – – ·	H · · · ·	I · ·	J · – – –	K – · –	L · – · ·
M – –	N – ·	O – – –	P · – – ·	Q – – · –	R · – ·
S · · ·	T –	U · · –	V · · · –	W · – –	X – · · –
Y – · – –	Z – – · ·				

Morse Code numbers:

1 · – – – –	2 · · – – –	3 · · · – –	4 · · · · –	5 · · · · ·
6 – · · · ·	7 – – · · ·	8 – – – · ·	9 – – – – ·	0 – – – – –

What do these messages say?

· · ·/– – –/· · ·

↓

[   ]

· ·   · · · ·/– – –/· – – ·/·   –/· · · ·/· –/ –   – · – –/– – –/· · –

· –/· – ·/·   ·/– ·/· – – –/– – –/ – · – – / · ·/– ·/– – ·

· · · ·/– – –/– –/·/· – –/– – –/· – ·/– ·   –/– – –/– · ·/· –/· · –

↓

[   ]

Now try writing your own message in Morse Code.

Name: Date:

Morse Code

In 1837, an American named Samuel Morse invented a system of sending messages through wires. This system was called the telegraph and was operated by sending electrical impulses along wires. The message had to be sent by using a special code, called Morse Code.

In Morse Code, letters are represented by dots and dashes. You can send Morse Code messages yourself by using a torch - quick flashes make the dots and longer flashes make the dashes. The most famous Morse Code signal is S.O.S., used by ships in distress.

Here is the Morse Code alphabet:

A · −   B − · · ·   C − · − ·   D − · ·   E ·   F · · − ·
G − − ·   H · · · ·   I · ·   J · − − −   K − · −   L · − · ·
M − −   N − ·   O − − −   P · − − ·   Q − − · −   R · − ·
S · · ·   T −   U · · −   V · · · −   W · − −   X − · · −
Y − · − −   Z − − · ·

Morse Code numbers:

1 · − − − −   2 · · − − −   3 · · · − −   4 · · · · −   5 · · · · ·
6 − · · · ·   7 − − · · ·   8 − − − · ·   9 − − − − ·   0 − − − − −

What do these messages say?

· · ·/− − −/· · ·

↓

| S O S |

· ·   · · · ·/− − −/· − − ·/· − − ·/   − /· · · ·/· − /−   − · − −/− − −/· · −
· − /· − ·/·   · /− · /· − − −/− − −/ − · − −   /· · /· − ·/· − · ·
· · · ·/− − −/− −/· · /− − −/− − −/· − ·/· − − /− − −/· · ·/· − ·/· − − −

↓

| I   HOPE   THAT   YOU |
| ARE   ENJOYING |
| HOMEWORK   TODAY |

Now try writing your own message in Morse Code.

© Andrew Brodie *Publications* ✓ PO Box 23, Wellington, Somerset, TA21 8YX ✓ www.andrewbrodie.co.uk

Name: Date:

Braille

In 1829 a Frenchman named Louis Braille invented a system of writing for blind people to read. It is known as the Braille alphabet. Each letter consists of a set of dots. These can be printed onto the paper by a press which raises the dots so that blind people can feel them with their fingers. The dot patterns are shown below but, on this paper, they are not raised up. Notice that some common words have their own dot pattern so that the writing is quicker to read.

The Braille Alphabet

A	B	C	D	E	F	G	H	I	J

K	L	M	N	O	P	Q	R	S	T

U	V	W	X	Y	Z		and	the	

Here is the name of a famous story. We have written it out using the Braille dot patterns. **Try to work out what the story is. One letter has been done for you.**

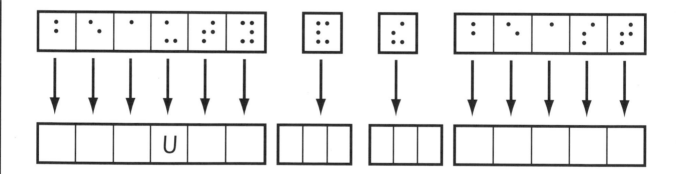

Louis Braille was blind himself.
See if you can find out how old he was when he went blind.
You may find this information in an encyclopedia.

Now write your own name using the Braille dot patterns:

Name: Date:

Braille

In 1829 a Frenchman named Louis Braille invented a system of writing for blind people to read. It is known as the Braille alphabet. Each letter consists of a set of dots. These can be printed onto the paper by a press which raises the dots so that blind people can feel them with their fingers. The dot patterns are shown below but, on this paper, they are not raised up. Notice that some common words have their own dot pattern so that the writing is quicker to read.

The Braille Alphabet

A   B   C   D   E   F   G   H   I   J

K   L   M   N   O   P   Q   R   S   T

U   V   W   X   Y   Z   and   the

Here is the name of a famous story. We have written it out using the Braille dot patterns. **Try to work out what the story is. One letter has been done for you.**

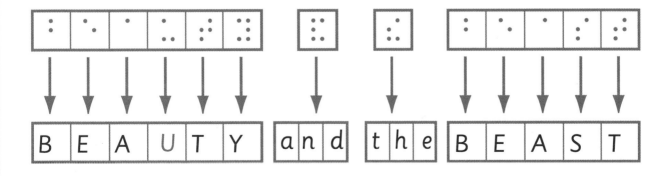

B E A U T Y   and   the   B E A S T

**Louis Braille was blind himself.
See if you can find out how old he was when he went blind.
You may find this information in an encyclopedia.**

Louis Braille was three years old when he went blind.

Now write your own name using the Braille dot patterns:

Name: Date:

Odd ones out

Draw a ring around the odd-one-out in each set. Write down, in note form, why it is the odd-one-out. The first one is done for you.

house   bungalow   shed   (town)   church

_ _ not a building _

dog   cat   rabbit   hamster   crocodile

_ _

envelope   eagle   elephant   eel   earwig

_ _

antelope   ant   lion   giraffe   elephant

_ _

ant   bee   ladybird   sparrow   beetle

_ _

London   Paris   Madrid   Rome   Manchester

_ _

New York   London   Birmingham   Edinburgh   Cardiff

_ _

_ _

_ _

_ _

3   15   4   9   19

_ _

Name: Date:

Odd ones out

Draw a ring around the odd-one-out in each set. Write down, in note form, why it is the odd-one-out. The first one is done for you.

house   bungalow   shed   (town)   church
_ _ _ not a building _ _ _ _ _ _ _ _ _ _ _ _ _ _ _ _ _ _ _

dog   cat   rabbit   hamster   (crocodile)
_ _ _ _ _ not a pet or not a mammal _ _ _ _ _ _ _ _

(envelope)   eagle   elephant   eel   earwig
_ _ _ _ not an animal _ _ _ _ _ _ _ _ _ _ _ _ _ _ _ _

antelope   (ant)   lion   giraffe   elephant
_ _ _ _ _ _ an insect, not a mammal _ _ _ _ _ _ _ _ _

ant   bee   ladybird   (sparrow)   beetle
_ _ _ _ _ _ a bird, not an insect _ _ _ _ _ _ _ _ _ _ _

London   Paris   Madrid   Rome   (Manchester)
_ _ _ _ _ _ _ _ _ _ _ not a capital city _ _ _ _ _ _ _

(New York)   London   Birmingham   Edinburgh   Cardiff
_ _ _ _ _ _ not in Britain _ _ _ _ _ _ _ _ _ _ _ _ _ _

an odd number, not even _ _ _ _ _ _ _ _ _ _ _ _ _ _

has no straight sides, or corners _ _ _ _ _ _ _ _ _

dot in middle, not in corner _ _ _ _ _ _ _ _ _ _ _ _

3   15   (4)   9   19
an even number, not odd _ _ _ _ _ _ _ _ _ _ _ _ _ _

© Andrew Brodie *Publications* ✓ PO Box 23, Wellington, Somerset, TA21 8YX ✓ www.andrewbrodie.co.uk

Cogs

Look at this pair of cogs...

When cog 1 turns clockwise it has the effect of making cog 2 turn anti-clockwise. The arrows show the directions of each cog.

A belt can make both wheels turn in the <u>same</u> direction.

On each set of cogs below, the direction of one cog is shown.
Draw arrows to show the direction of movement of the other cogs.

1.

2.

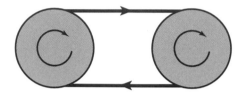

3.

4.

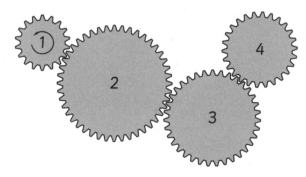

5.

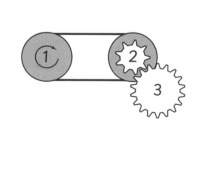

6.

7.

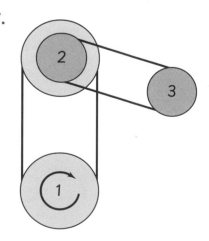

© Andrew Brodie *Publications* ✓ PO Box 23, Wellington, Somerset, TA21 8YX ✓ www.andrewbrodie.co.uk

Name: Date:

Cogs

Look at this pair of cogs...

When cog 1 turns clockwise it has the effect of making cog 2 turn anti-clockwise. The arrows show the directions of each cog.

A belt can make both wheels turn in the <u>same</u> direction.

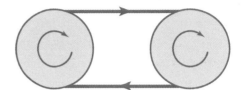

On each set of cogs below, the direction of one cog is shown.
Draw arrows to show the direction of movement of the other cogs.

1.

2.

3.

4.

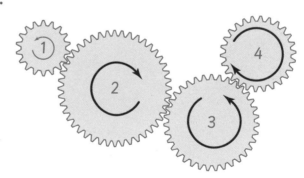

5.

6.

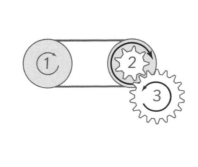

7.

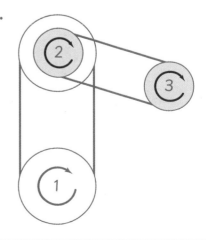

© Andrew Brodie *Publications* ✓ PO Box 23, Wellington, Somerset, TA21 8YX ✓ www.andrewbrodie.co.uk

Name: Date:

The Planets There are 9 planets which travel around the sun.
With the picture of each planet is its approximate distance from the sun.

The picture makes it look as though the planets are close together but they are actually millions of kilometres apart.

Venus
108 million kilometres from the sun.
12140 kilometres in diameter.

Mars
228 million kilometres from the sun.
6790 kilometres in diameter.

Pluto
5900 million kilometres from the sun.
2300 kilometres in diameter.

Uranus
2870 million kilometres from the sun.
51000 kilometres in diameter.

The Sun

Jupiter
778 million kilometres from the sun.
142600 kilometres in diameter

Saturn
1427 million kilometres from the sun.

Earth
150 million kilometres from the sun.
12750 kilometres in diameter.

120200 kilometres in diameter

Neptune
4497 million kilometres from the sun.
49000 kilometres in diameter.

Mercury
58 million kilometres from the sun.
4850 kilometres in diameter.

Use the information about the planets to solve this puzzle…

Clues Across:
1. Diameter: 142600 km
2. 4497 million kilometres from the sun.
3. 4th closest to the sun.
4. Letter 'u' appears twice in its name.

Clues Down:
1. 1427 million kilometres from the sun.
2. Furthest from the sun.
3. Closest to the sun.
4. Diameter: 12140 km
5. Where we live, 150 million kilometres from the sun.

The Planets

There are 9 planets which travel around the sun.
With the picture of each planet is its approximate distance from the sun.

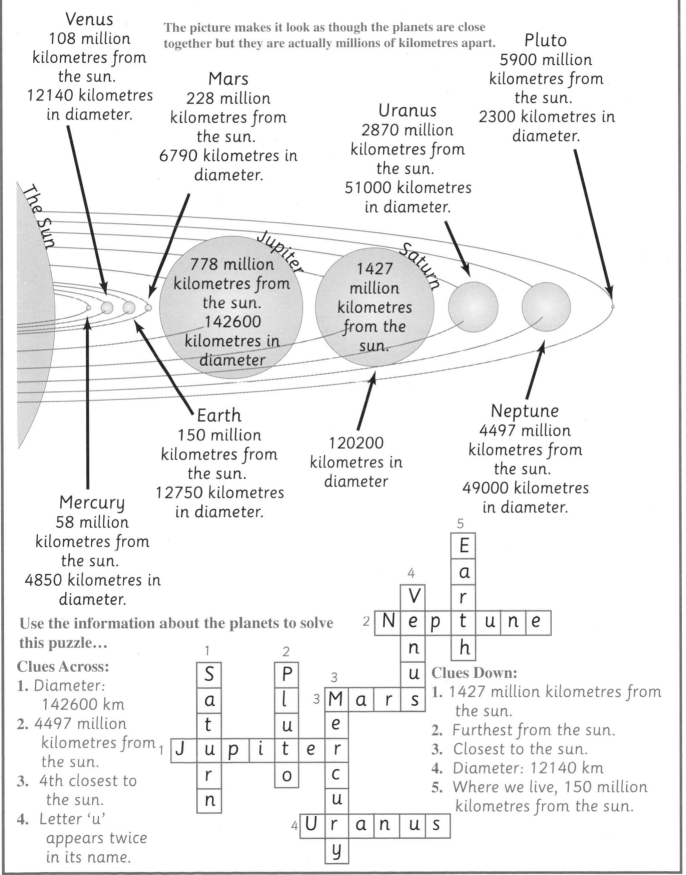

Venus
108 million kilometres from the sun.
12140 kilometres in diameter.

The picture makes it look as though the planets are close together but they are actually millions of kilometres apart.

Mars
228 million kilometres from the sun.
6790 kilometres in diameter.

Pluto
5900 million kilometres from the sun.
2300 kilometres in diameter.

Uranus
2870 million kilometres from the sun.
51000 kilometres in diameter.

The Sun

Jupiter
778 million kilometres from the sun.
142600 kilometres in diameter

Saturn
1427 million kilometres from the sun.

Earth
150 million kilometres from the sun.
12750 kilometres in diameter.

120200 kilometres in diameter

Neptune
4497 million kilometres from the sun.
49000 kilometres in diameter.

Mercury
58 million kilometres from the sun.
4850 kilometres in diameter.

Use the information about the planets to solve this puzzle...

Clues Across:
1. Diameter: 142600 km
2. 4497 million kilometres from the sun.
3. 4th closest to the sun.
4. Letter 'u' appears twice in its name.

Clues Down:
1. 1427 million kilometres from the sun.
2. Furthest from the sun.
3. Closest to the sun.
4. Diameter: 12140 km
5. Where we live, 150 million kilometres from the sun.

Crossword answers:
- 5 Down: E a r t h
- 4 Down: V e n u s
- 2 Across: N e p t u n e
- 1 Down: S a t u r n
- 2 Down: P l u t o
- 3 Across: M a r s
- 3 Down: M e r c u r y
- 1 Across: J u p i t e r
- 4 Across: U r a n u s

© Andrew Brodie *Publications* ✓ PO Box 23, Wellington, Somerset, TA21 8YX ✓ www.andrewbrodie.co.uk

Name: Date:

Earth and Sun

Every day, the Earth spins around once on its own axis.
From Earth it looks as if the sun is moving across the sky.
On the picture below, draw the approximate positions of the sun in the mid-afternoon and in the late evening.

Mid-day

Mid-morning

Sun

Early morning

A stick in the ground would have a long shadow in the early morning. The shadow would be in a different position and shorter at mid-morning.

Draw shadows as they would appear in the mid-afternoon and in the late evening.

In London on 19th December the sun rises at 08:03 and sets at 15:53.

These times are shown in 24-hour clock notation.
What time does the sun set according to the 12-hour clock?

How many hours and minutes of daylight are there from sunrise to noon on 19th December?

How many hours and minutes of daylight are there from noon until sunset on 19th December?

Altogether, how many hours and minutes of daylight are there in London on 19th December?

On 20th June in London, the sun rises at 04:43 and sets at 21:21.

Work out the setting time in the 12-hour clock:

How many hours and minutes it is from sunrise until noon?

How many hours and minutes it is from noon until sunset?

Find the total hours and minutes of daylight on 20th June:

How much more daylight is there on 20th June than 19th December?

Earth and Sun

Every day, the Earth spins around once on its own axis.
From Earth it looks as if the sun is moving across the sky.
On the picture below, draw the approximate positions of the sun in
the mid-afternoon and in the late evening.

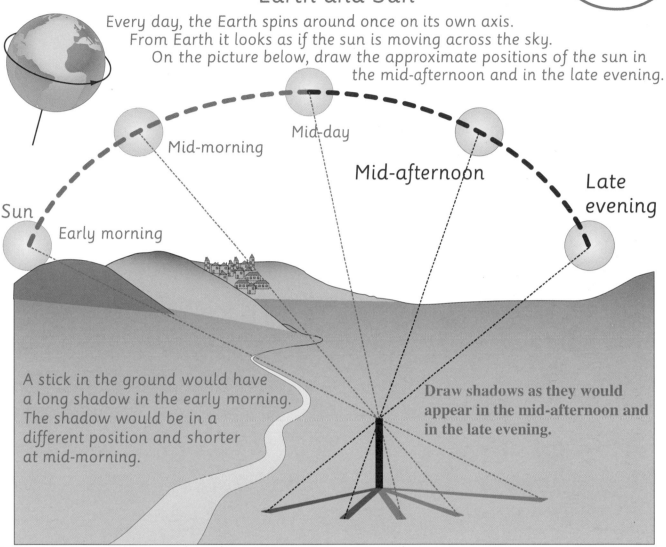

Mid-morning

Mid-day

Mid-afternoon

Late evening

Sun

Early morning

A stick in the ground would have a long shadow in the early morning. The shadow would be in a different position and shorter at mid-morning.

Draw shadows as they would appear in the mid-afternoon and in the late evening.

In London on 19th December the sun rises at 08:03 and sets at 15:53.
These times are shown in 24-hour clock notation.
What time does the sun set according to the 12-hour clock? | **3·53 p.m.**

How many hours and minutes of daylight are there
from sunrise to noon on 19th December? | **3hrs 57mins**

How many hours and minutes of daylight are there
from noon until sunset on 19th December? | **3hrs 53 mins**

Altogether, how many hours and minutes of daylight
are there in London on 19th December? | **7hrs 50mins**

On 20th June in London, the sun rises at 04:43 and sets at 21:21.

Work out the setting time in the 12-hour clock: | **9·21 p.m**

How many hours and minutes it is from sunrise until noon? | **7hrs 17mins**

How many hours and minutes it is from noon until sunset? | **9hrs 21 mins**

Find the total hours and minutes of daylight on 20th June: | **16hrs 38mins**

How much more daylight is there on 20th June than 19th December? | **8hrs 48mins**

© Andrew Brodie *Publications* ✓ PO Box 23, Wellington, Somerset, TA21 8YX ✓ www.andrewbrodie.co.uk

Food Chains

In science we call green plants '<u>producers</u>'.

Rabbits eat grass so we say that rabbits are '<u>first order consumers</u>'.

Buzzards eat rabbits so we say that buzzards are '<u>second order consumers</u>'.

We also describe the buzzards as predators and the rabbits as prey.

Buzzards
eat
Rabbits

Rabbits
eat
Grass

Here is another food chain:

What is the producer?

_____

Which are the consumers?

_____

_____

Which do you think is the second order consumer?

_____

Which do you think is the third order consumer?

_____

Sparrowhawk

↑

Hedge
Sparrow

↑

Caterpillar

↑

Stinging
nettle

The sparrowhawk preys on the
hedge sparrow so we call it a _____ .

On the back of the sheet, draw and label a simple food chain with you at the top. Remember that food chains start with green plants.

Name: Date:

Food Chains

In science we call green plants '<u>producers</u>'.

Rabbits eat grass so we say that rabbits are '<u>first order consumers</u>'.

Buzzards eat rabbits so we say that buzzards are '<u>second order consumers</u>'.

We also describe the buzzards as predators and the rabbits as prey.

Buzzards
eat
Rabbits

Rabbits
eat
Grass

Here is another food chain:

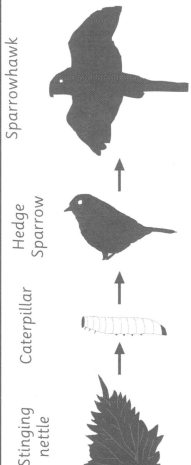

Sparrowhawk

Hedge
Sparrow

Caterpillar

Stinging
nettle

What is the producer?

The stinging nettle.

Which are the consumers?

The caterpillar, the hedge sparrow and

the sparrowhawk.

Which do you think is the second order consumer?

The hedge sparrow.

Which do you think is the third order consumer?

The sparrowhawk.

The sparrowhawk preys on the
hedge sparrow so we call it a _____ predator. ____.

**On the back of the sheet, draw and label a simple food chain with
you at the top. Remember that food chains start with green plants.**

© Andrew Brodie *Publications* ✓ PO Box 23, Wellington, Somerset, TA21 8YX ✓ www.andrewbrodie.co.uk

Plan of a School

Main Entrance
Secretary's Office
Head's Office

Miss Green's Class

Hall

Store

Mrs. Thorn's Class

N

Miss Winn's Class

Library and Shared Work Area

Staff Room

Mr. Lee's Class

Boys' Toilets

Girls' Toilets

Mrs. Ward's Class

Mrs. Smith's Class

Scale: 1 cm : 4 m

On the plan, Miss Winn's classroom is shown as 3 cm wide.

What is the actual width of the classroom?

Measure with a ruler then work out the actual dimensions of the following rooms:

The hall: by

The Staff Room: by

The Head's Office: by

Miss Green's Classroom: by

Mrs. Thorn's Classroom: by

The pupils in Miss Green's class get wet on a rainy day when they come into the main school building. Approximately how many metres do they have to walk from the classroom to the main entrance?

What is the area of the school hall?

© Andrew Brodie *Publications* ✓ PO Box 23, Wellington, Somerset, TA21 8YX ✓ www.andrewbrodie.co.uk

Name: Date:

Plan of a School

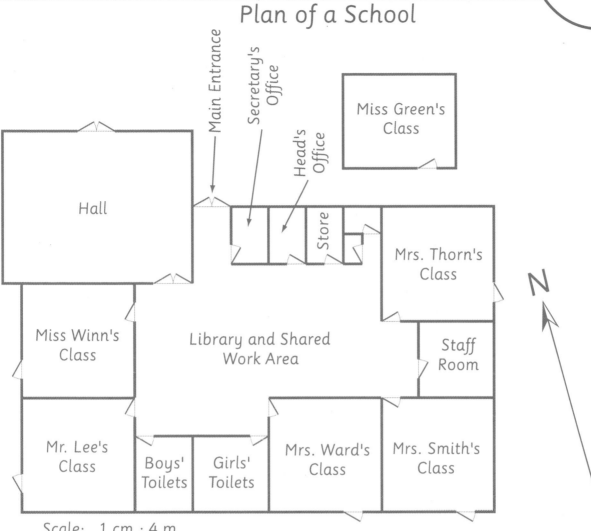

Scale: 1 cm : 4 m

On the plan, Miss Winn's classroom is shown as 3 cm wide.

What is the actual width of the classroom? | 12 m |

Measure with a ruler then work out the actual dimensions of the following rooms:

The hall:	20 m	by	16 m
The Staff Room:	8 m	by	8 m
The Head's Office:	4 m	by	6 m
Miss Green's Classroom:	12 m	by	10 m
Mrs. Thorn's Classroom:	12 m	by	12 m

The pupils in Miss Green's class get wet on a rainy day when they come into the main school building. Approximately how many metres do they have to walk from the classroom to the main entrance? | 24 m |

What is the area of the school hall? | 320 m² |

© Andrew Brodie *Publications* ✓ PO Box 23, Wellington, Somerset, TA21 8YX ✓ www.andrewbrodie.co.uk

Homework Today

Name: Date:

Using a map

Here is part of a map:

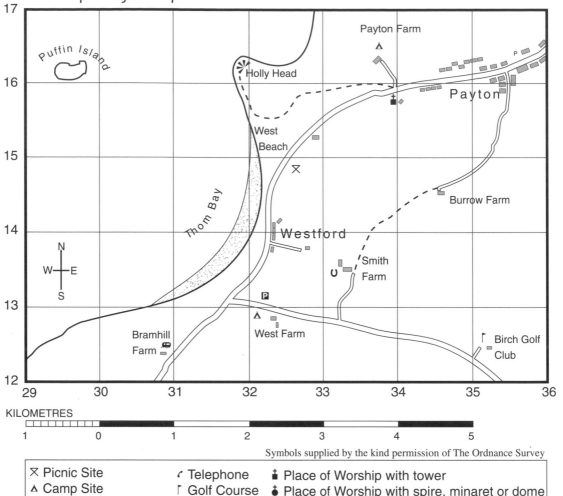

Symbols supplied by the kind permission of The Ordnance Survey

☒ Picnic Site	✆ Telephone	♟ Place of Worship with tower
⛺ Camp Site	⌐ Golf Course	♦ Place of Worship with spire, minaret or dome
🚐 Caravan Site	⊡ Parking	+ Place of Worship without tower or spire
⚔ Battlefield (with date) 1066	ₚ Post Office	℧ Riding Establishment
🔭Viewpoint		
	- - - - - - - - - Permitted Path	══════ Road

1. At which farm could you go riding? _____

2. Opposite which building would you find a footpath to Holly Head? _____

3. At which farm could you stay in a caravan?_____

4. At which farms could you camp?_____

5. What special feature does the church have?_____

6. In which village is the Post Office?_____

7. Which farm will you come to if you walk in a south-westerly

      direction from Burrow Farm?_____

8. Colour the sea blue.   9.   Colour the roads red.

10. Use other colours to complete the map.

© Andrew Brodie *Publications* ✓ PO Box 23, Wellington, Somerset, TA21 8YX ✓ www.andrewbrodie.co.uk

Name: _____ Date: _____

Using a map

Here is part of a map:

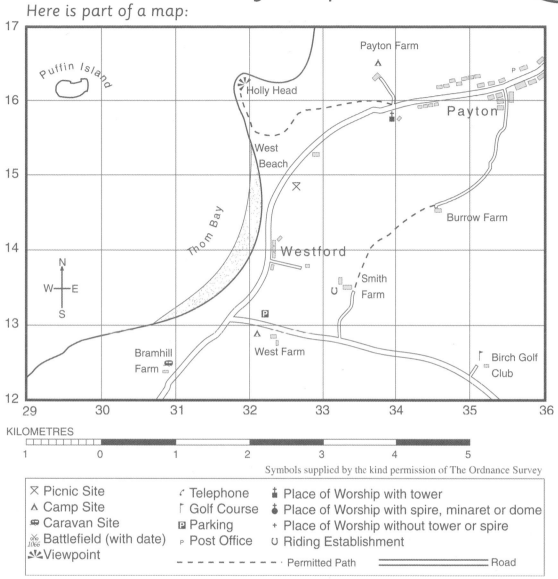

KILOMETRES

1 0 1 2 3 4 5

Symbols supplied by the kind permission of The Ordnance Survey

✗ Picnic Site	☎ Telephone	⛩ Place of Worship with tower
⅄ Camp Site	⌐ Golf Course	⛪ Place of Worship with spire, minaret or dome
⚏ Caravan Site	⊡ Parking	+ Place of Worship without tower or spire
⚔ Battlefield (with date)	P Post Office	↻ Riding Establishment
1066		
⩘Viewpoint	- - - - - Permitted Path	══════ Road

1. At which farm could you go riding? **Smith Farm**

2. Opposite which building would you find a footpath to Holly Head? **Payton Church**

3. At which farm could you stay in a caravan? **Bramhill Farm**

4. At which farms could you camp? **West Farm and Payton Farm**

5. What special feature does the church have? **A tower**

6. In which village is the Post Office? **Payton**

7. Which farm will you come to if you walk in a south-westerly
   direction from Burrow Farm? **Smith Farm**

8. Colour the sea blue.   9. Colour the roads red.

10. Use other colours to complete the map.

© Andrew Brodie *Publications* ✓ PO Box 23, Wellington, Somerset, TA21 8YX ✓ www.andrewbrodie.co.uk

Homework Today

Name: Date:

Grid References

Symbols supplied by the kind permission of The Ordnance Survey

⚊ Picnic Site	
⋀ Camp Site	
Caravan Site	
Battlefield (with date) 1066	
Viewpoint	
☏ Telephone	
Golf Course	
Ⓟ Parking	
P Post Office	
Place of Worship with tower	
Place of Worship with spire, minaret or dome	
+ Place of Worship without tower or spire	
∪ Riding Establishment	
– – – – – Permitted Path	
══════ Road	

We can use grid references to explain where places are on the map. Four-figure grid references are used to identify the lower left hand corner of a square. For example, we say that Smith Farm is in square 33 13.

Look <u>across</u> the page to find the first number.   Look <u>up</u> the page to find the second number.

Give the four figure grid reference for the following places:

Burrow Farm ☐☐   Payton Farm ☐☐   Puffin Island ☐☐

Birch Golf Club ☐☐   The car park ☐☐   The picnic site ☐☐

Draw symbols for the following extra features on the map:

A caravan site in square 33 12

A public telephone in square 35 16

A battlefield dated 1645 in square 34 13

A campsite in square 29 16 (be careful where you put this one!)

A place of worship without a tower, spire, minaret or dome in the hamlet of Westford in square 32 13

© Andrew Brodie *Publications* ✔ PO Box 23, Wellington, Somerset, TA21 8YX ✔ www.andrewbrodie.co.uk

Name: Date:

Grid References

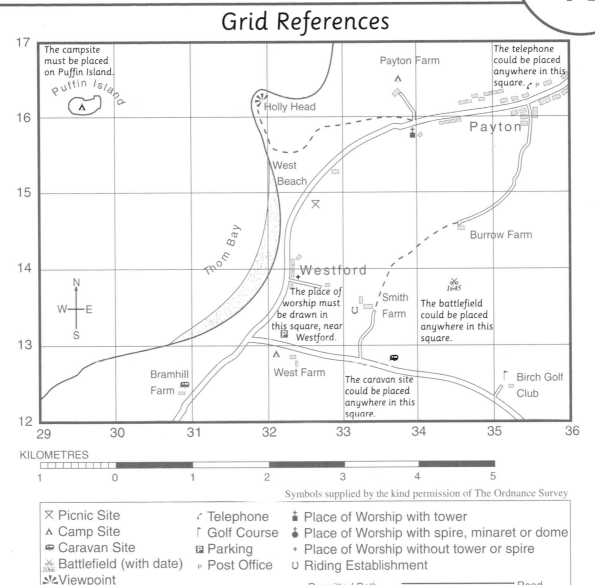

Symbols supplied by the kind permission of The Ordnance Survey

⊠ Picnic Site
∧ Camp Site
⛟ Caravan Site
⚔ Battlefield (with date)
🔭 Viewpoint

ʕ Telephone
Γ Golf Course
🅿 Parking
P Post Office

♜ Place of Worship with tower
♟ Place of Worship with spire, minaret or dome
+ Place of Worship without tower or spire
U Riding Establishment

– – – – – Permitted Path   ═══════ Road

We can use grid references to explain where places are on the map. Four-figure grid references are used to identify the lower left hand corner of a square. For example, we say that Smith Farm is in square 33 13.

Look **across** the page to find the first number.   Look **up** the page to find the second number.

Give the four figure grid reference for the following places:

Burrow Farm ⟨34⟩⟨14⟩   Payton Farm ⟨33⟩⟨16⟩   Puffin Island ⟨29⟩⟨16⟩

Birch Golf Club ⟨35⟩⟨12⟩   The car park ⟨32⟩⟨13⟩   The picnic site ⟨32⟩⟨14⟩

Draw symbols for the following extra features on the map:
    A caravan site in square 33 12
    A public telephone in square 35 16
    A battlefield dated 1645 in square 34 13
    A campsite in square 29 16 (be careful where you put this one!)
    A place of worship without a tower, spire, minaret or dome in the hamlet of
        Westford in square 32 13

© Andrew Brodie *Publications* ✓ PO Box 23, Wellington, Somerset, TA21 8YX ✓ www.andrewbrodie.co.uk

Name: Date:

Using the scale 1

Symbols supplied by the kind permission of The Ordnance Survey

✕ Picnic Site	⌒ Telephone	♗ Place of Worship with tower
▲ Camp Site	⌐ Golf Course	♙ Place of Worship with spire, minaret or dome
⇌ Caravan Site	℗ Parking	+ Place of Worship without tower or spire
※₁₀₆₆ Battlefield (with date)	ₚ Post Office	∪ Riding Establishment
♯ Viewpoint		
- - - - - - - - Permitted Path		══════ Road

You can see that the map is drawn to a scale of 2 cm : 1 km.
This means that 2 cm on the map represents 1 km.

...so 1 cm would show $\frac{1}{2}$ km or 500 m.

Use a ruler to measure the distances listed below. Give your answers to the nearest centimetre then work out the actual distances that your measurements represent.

From Bramhill Farm to Birch Golf Club: [ ] cm ⟶ [ ] km

From Holly Head to the West side of Puffin Island: [ ] cm ⟶ [ ] km

From Bramhill Farm to the Post Office: [ ] cm ⟶ [ ] km

From the Holly Head Viewpoint to Payton Church: [ ] cm ⟶ [ ] km

The distances you have measured have all been straight lines, 'as the crow flies'. Use a piece of string or wool to try to find the distance from the Viewpoint to the Church. Lay the piece of string carefully along the footpath then measure the string you have used to do this.

Length of string used from the Viewpoint to the Church: [ ] cm

Approximate distance in kilometres: [ ] km

Name: Date:

Using the scale 1

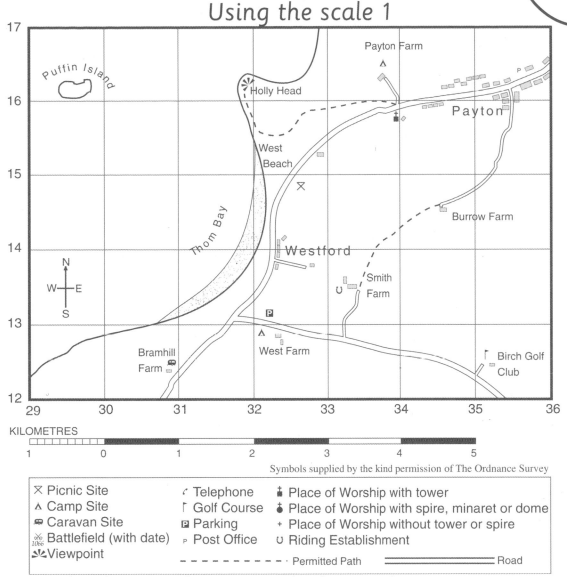

Symbols supplied by the kind permission of The Ordnance Survey

✕	Picnic Site	⌐	Telephone	▄	Place of Worship with tower
⌂	Camp Site	Γ	Golf Course	♠	Place of Worship with spire, minaret or dome
🚐	Caravan Site	⊡	Parking	+	Place of Worship without tower or spire
⚔ 1066	Battlefield (with date)	P	Post Office	∪	Riding Establishment
⩘	Viewpoint				

- - - - - - - · Permitted Path   ══════ Road

You can see that the map is drawn to a scale of 2 cm : 1 km.
This means that 2 cm on the map represents 1 km.

...so 1 cm would show $\frac{1}{2}$ km or 500 m.

Use a ruler to measure the distances listed below. Give your answers to the nearest centimetre then work out the actual distances that your measurements represent.

From Bramhill Farm to Birch Golf Club: 9 cm → 4·5 km

From Holly Head to the West side of Puffin Island: 5 cm → 2·5 km

From Bramhill Farm to the Post Office: 12 cm → 6 km

From the Holly Head Viewpoint to Payton Church: 4 cm → 2 km

The distances you have measured have all been straight lines, 'as the crow flies'. Use a piece of string or wool to try to find the distance from the Viewpoint to the Church. Lay the piece of string carefully along the footpath then measure the string you have used to do this.

Length of string used from the Viewpoint to the Church: 6 cm

Approximate distance in kilometres: 3 km

Name: Date:

Compass Directions

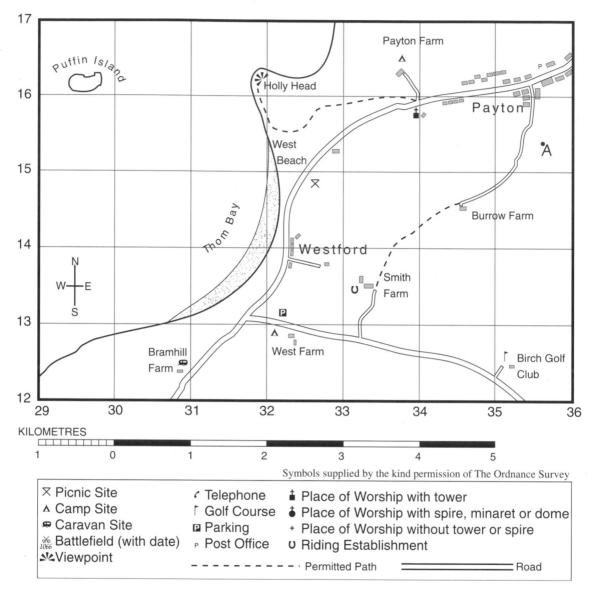

Mark the letters below on your map.
The first one is done for you.

<u>Letter A</u>, 1 km south of Payton Post Office.
<u>Letter B</u>, 3 km west of Payton Church.
<u>Letter C</u>, 2 km south of Puffin Island.
<u>Letter D</u>, 1·5 km north of the Caravan Site.
<u>Letter E</u>, 2·5 km east of the Picnic Site.
<u>Letter F</u>, 1 km south-east of Puffin Island.
<u>Letter G</u>, 3 km north-west of Burrow Farm.
<u>Letter H</u>, 0·5 km north-east of the Car Park.
<u>Letter I</u>, 2 km south-west of Holly Head Viewpoint.

Remember that
the map is drawn to a
scale in which 2 cm
represents 1 km.

Name: Date:

Compass Directions

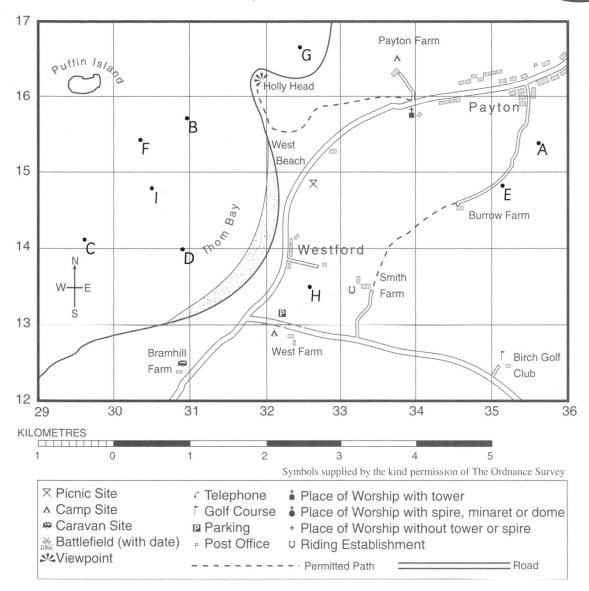

Symbols supplied by the kind permission of The Ordnance Survey

⊠ Picnic Site	☏ Telephone	⌘ Place of Worship with tower
Λ Camp Site	Γ Golf Course	♦ Place of Worship with spire, minaret or dome
⌂ Caravan Site	℗ Parking	+ Place of Worship without tower or spire
⚔ Battlefield (with date) 1066	P Post Office	℧ Riding Establishment
⚘ Viewpoint	- - - - - Permitted Path	══════ Road

Mark the letters below on your map.
The first one is done for you.

Letter A, 1 km south of Payton Post Office.

Letter B, 3 km west of Payton Church.

Letter C, 2 km south of Puffin Island.

Letter D, 1·5 km north of the Caravan Site.

Letter E, 2·5 km east of the Picnic Site.

Letter F, 1 km south-east of Puffin Island.

Letter G, 3 km north-west of Burrow Farm.

Letter H, 0·5 km north-east of the Car Park.

Letter I, 2 km south-west of Holly Head Viewpoint.

Remember that the map is drawn to a scale in which 2 cm represents 1 km.

The British Isles

Mark the following places on the map:

Atlantic Ocean
English Channel
Irish Sea
North Sea

England
Northern Ireland
Republic of Ireland
Scotland
Wales

Shade the sea blue and shade each country a different colour.

MAP © MAPS IN MINUTES™ (1998)

N

| 0 | | 50 Miles |
| 0 | | 80 Km |

© Andrew Brodie *Publications* ✓ PO Box 23, Wellington, Somerset, TA21 8YX ✓ www.andrewbrodie.co.uk

Name: Date:

The British Isles

Mark the following places on the map:

Atlantic Ocean
English Channel
Irish Sea
North Sea

England
Northern Ireland
Republic of Ireland
Scotland
Wales

Shade the sea blue and shade each country a different colour.

North Sea

Scotland

Atlantic
Ocean

Northern
Ireland

Irish
Sea

Republic
of
Ireland

England

Wales

MAP © MAPS IN MINUTES™ (1998)

N

| 0 | | 50 Miles |
| 0 | | 80 Km |

English Channel

Some Towns and Cities

Mark on the map each of the towns and cities which are
listed below.
Answer spaces are provided for you. If your local town is
not listed, you could mark that one on as well.

Aberdeen   Norwich
Belfast   Nottingham
Birmingham   Plymouth
Bristol   Sheffield
Cambridge   Southampton
Cardiff   Swansea
Cork   York
Dublin
Edinburgh
Glasgow
Hull
Inverness
Leeds
London
Liverpool
Manchester
Newcastle-upon-Tyne

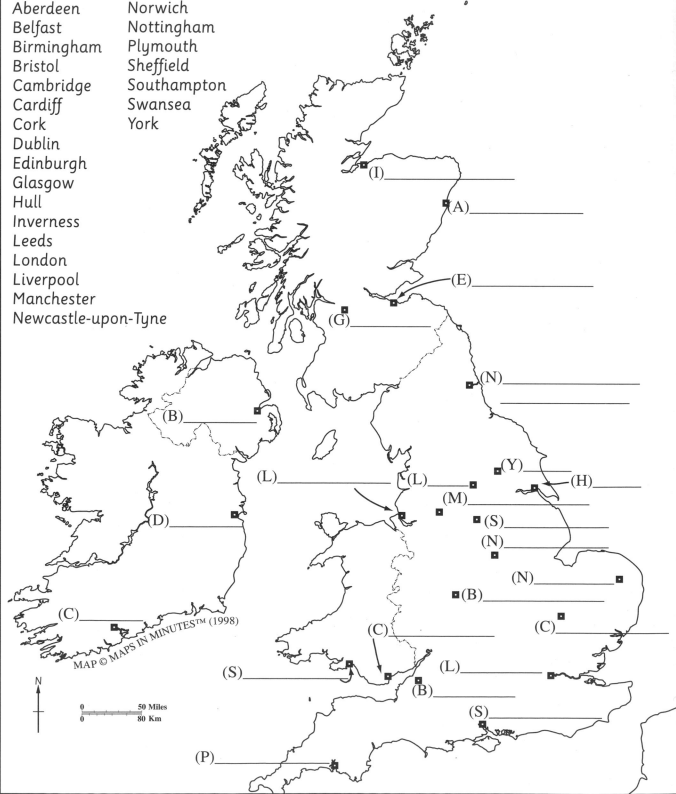

(I)_____

(A)_____

(E)_____

(G)_____

(N)_____
_____

(B)_____

(Y)_____

(L)_____   (L)_____   (H)_____

(M)_____

(S)_____

(D)_____

(N)_____

(N)_____

(B)_____

(C)_____

(C)_____

(S)_____

(L)_____

(B)_____

(S)_____

(P)_____

MAP © MAPS IN MINUTES™ (1998)

N

0   50 Miles
0   80 Km

© Andrew Brodie *Publications* ✓ PO Box 23, Wellington, Somerset, TA21 8YX ✓ www.andrewbrodie.co.uk

Name: Date:

Some Towns and Cities

Mark on the map each of the towns and cities which are listed below.

Answer spaces are provided for you. If your local town is not listed, you could mark that one on as well.

Aberdeen   Norwich
Belfast   Nottingham
Birmingham   Plymouth
Bristol   Sheffield
Cambridge   Southampton
Cardiff   Swansea
Cork   York
Dublin
Edinburgh
Glasgow
Hull
Inverness
Leeds
London
Liverpool
Manchester
Newcastle-upon-Tyne

(I) Inverness

(A) Aberdeen

(E) Edinburgh

(G) Glasgow

(N) Newcastle-upon-Tyne

(B) Belfast

(L) Liverpool   (L) Leeds   (Y) York   (H) Hull

(M) Manchester

(D) Dublin   (S) Sheffield

(N) Nottingham

(N) Norwich

(B) Birmingham

(C) Cork   (C) Cambridge

(C) Cardiff

(S) Swansea   (L) London

(B) Bristol

(S) Southampton

(P) Plymouth

MAP © MAPS IN MINUTES™ (1998)

N

0   50 Miles
0   80 Km

Using the scale 2

The scale on this map is 2 cm : 100 km.
    ...so every centimetre
    must represent 50 km.

**Find the distances in the box
opposite on the map to the
nearest half-centimetre
'as the crow flies'.
Then work out the actual
distance in kilometres.**

John O'Groats

Inverness

Edinburgh

Glasgow

Belfast

Dublin

Birmingham

London

Plymouth

Land's End

N

| 0 | | 50 Miles |
| 0 | | 80 Km |

MAP © MAPS IN MINUTES™ (1998)

Dublin to Belfast:

| 3cm | ➔ | 150km |

Belfast to Edinburgh:

| | ➔ | |

Edinburgh to Inverness:

| | ➔ | |

Glasgow to Birmingham:

| | ➔ | |

Dublin to London:

| | ➔ | |

Plymouth to Inverness:

| | ➔ | |

Land's End to John O'Groats:

| | ➔ | |

Name: Date:

Using the scale 2

The scale on this map is 2 cm : 100 km.
   ...so every centimetre
   must represent 50 km.

**Find the distances in the box
opposite on the map to the
nearest half-centimetre
'as the crow flies'.
Then work out the actual
distance in kilometres.**

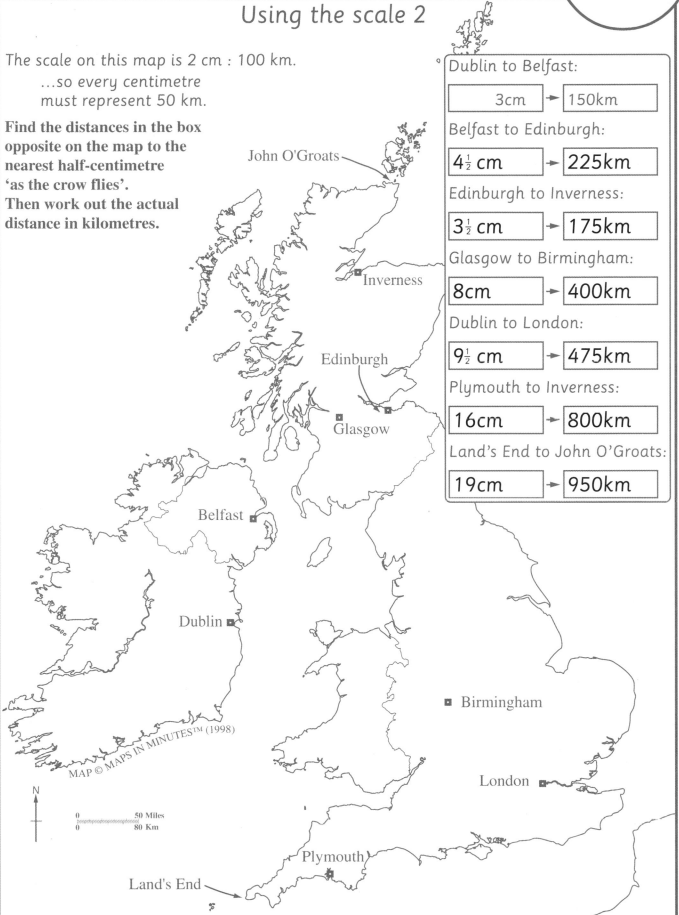

Dublin to Belfast:

| 3cm | ➜ | 150km |

Belfast to Edinburgh:

| $4\frac{1}{2}$ cm | ➜ | 225km |

Edinburgh to Inverness:

| $3\frac{1}{2}$ cm | ➜ | 175km |

Glasgow to Birmingham:

| 8cm | ➜ | 400km |

Dublin to London:

| $9\frac{1}{2}$ cm | ➜ | 475km |

Plymouth to Inverness:

| 16cm | ➜ | 800km |

Land's End to John O'Groats:

| 19cm | ➜ | 950km |

John O'Groats

Inverness

Edinburgh

Glasgow

Belfast

Dublin

Birmingham

London

MAP © MAPS IN MINUTES™ (1998)

N

| 0 | 50 Miles |
| 0 | 80 Km |

Plymouth

Land's End

On this map, mark the following places:

England   The Lake District
Scotland   The Pennines
Wales   The Grampian Mountains
Northern Ireland   The Cambrian Mountains

London   The English Channel
Edinburgh   The Irish Sea
Cardiff
Belfast

River Trent
River Severn
River Thames

Shade the sea in blue.
Shade the land in green.

United Kingdom:
Points of reference

MAP © MAPS IN MINUTES™ (1998)

0   50 Miles
0   80 Km

N

Name: Date:

On this map, mark the following places:

England   The Lake District
Scotland   The Pennines
Wales   The Grampian Mountains
Northern Ireland   The Cambrian Mountains

London   The English Channel
Edinburgh   The Irish Sea
Cardiff
Belfast

River Trent
River Severn
River Thames

Shade the sea in blue.
Shade the land in green.

United Kingdom:
Points of reference

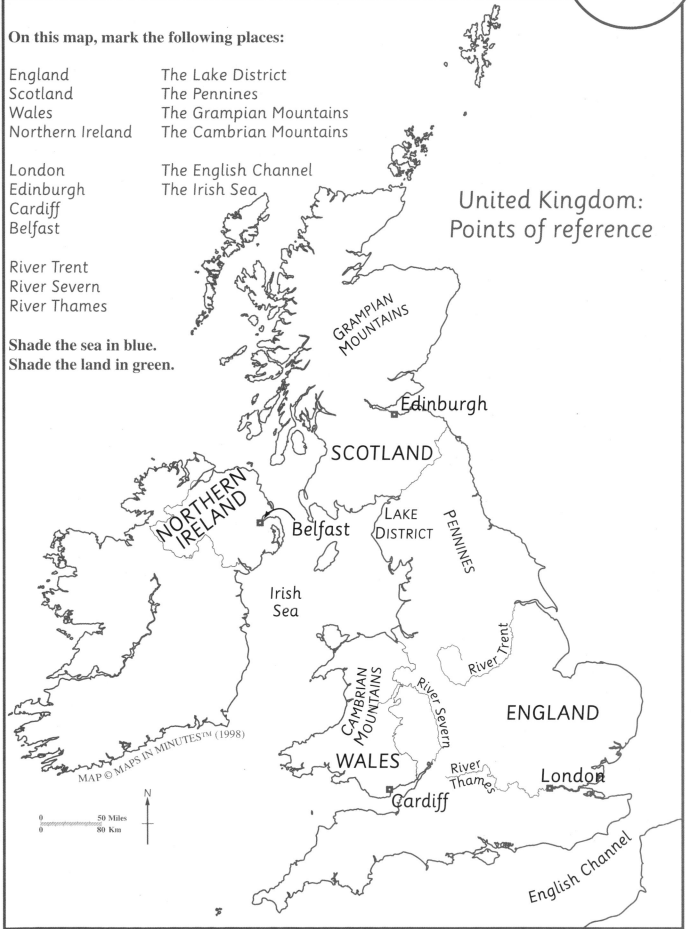

GRAMPIAN MOUNTAINS

Edinburgh

SCOTLAND

NORTHERN IRELAND

Belfast

LAKE DISTRICT

PENNINES

Irish Sea

River Trent

CAMBRIAN MOUNTAINS

River Severn

ENGLAND

WALES

River Thames

Cardiff

London

MAP © MAPS IN MINUTES™ (1998)

N

0   50 Miles
0   80 Km

English Channel

© Andrew Brodie *Publications* ✓ PO Box 23, Wellington, Somerset, TA21 8YX ✓ www.andrewbrodie.co.uk

Homework Today

Name: Date:

Which motorway goes all the way around London? [   ]

Which motorway connects Wales to London? [   ]

Which motorway links Glasgow to Edinburgh? [   ]

If I travelled from Exeter to London, which motorways would I use? [   ] [   ]

If I travelled from Cardiff to Cambridge by motorway, which ones would I use?

[   ] [   ] [   ]

If I travelled from London to Oxford, which motorway would I use? [   ]

If I travelled from Hull to Liverpool, which motorway would I use? [   ]

Motorway Routes

MAP © MAPS IN MINUTES™ (1998)

0   50 Miles
0   80 Km

© Andrew Brodie *Publications* ✔ PO Box 23, Wellington, Somerset, TA21 8YX ✔ www.andrewbrodie.co.uk

Name: Date:

Which motorway goes all the way around London? | M25 |

Which motorway connects Wales to London? | M4 |

Which motorway links Glasgow to Edinburgh? | M8 |

If I travelled from Exeter to London, which
motorways would I use? | M5 | | M4 |

If I travelled from Cardiff to
Cambridge by motorway,
which ones would I use?

| M4 | | M25 | | M11 |

If I travelled from
London to Oxford,
which motorway
would I use? | M40 |

If I travelled from Hull to
Liverpool, which motorway
would I use? | M62 |

Motorway Routes

Edinburgh

M9 M90 M8
M8 M9
M74
Glasgow

A74(M)

M6
A1(M)

M6
A1(M)
Hull

M6
M62 M62
Liverpool
M1

M6
M1

M54 M42
M6 M42
M42 M6
M1
A1(M)
Cambridge

M50
M40
M1
A1(M) M11
M25
Cardiff M5 Oxford
M4 M4 M4 London
M4 M25
M3 M25 M2
M25 M23 M20

M27

Exeter

M2
M2
M1

M1

M4 M7
M7
M9

0   50 Miles
0   80 Km

MAP © MAPS IN MINUTES™ (1998)

© Andrew Brodie *Publications* ✓ PO Box 23, Wellington, Somerset, TA21 8YX ✓ www.andrewbrodie.co.uk

Name: Date:

Timeline: 0 to 1000

Our dating system begins with the year 0. Dates of years after this are known as 'A.D.' which is short for 'Anno Domini', meaning 'the year of our Lord'. Dates before the year 0 are known as B.C. which stands for 'Before Christ'. Historians now believe, however, that Jesus was probably born before the year 0, perhaps in the year 5 B.C.

Here is a list of some important events from the year 5 B.C. to the year 1000. They are not listed in order. Put them in order by neatly writing them in the appropriate places next to the time line.

<u>844 A.D.</u> - Kenneth MacAlpine becomes King of Scotland.

<u>605 A.D. - 610 A.D.</u> - Grand Canal built in China.

<u>432 A.D.</u> - St. Patrick takes Christianity to Ireland.

<u>122 A.D.</u> - Hadrian's Wall started.

<u>757 A.D.</u> - Offa builds Offa's Dyke between England and Wales.

<u>250 A.D.</u> - Roman Emperor orders persecution of Christians.

<u>861 A.D.</u> - Vikings discover Iceland.

<u>370 A.D.</u> - Europe invaded by Huns from Asia.

<u>407 A.D.</u> - Last Roman troops leave Britain.

<u>58 A.D.</u> - Buddhism introduced to China.

<u>570 A.D.</u> - Muhammad born in Mecca.

<u>630 A.D.</u> - Muhammad states the principles of Islam.

<u>5 B.C.</u> - Birth of Jesus

<u>550 A.D.</u> - St. David introduces Christianity to Wales.

<u>981 A.D.</u> - Eric the Red, a Viking, settles in Greenland.

<u>77 A.D.</u> - Romans conquer Britain.

<u>937 A.D.</u> - Athelstan claims to be King of Scotland.

<u>787 A.D.</u> - Britain attacked by Danes.

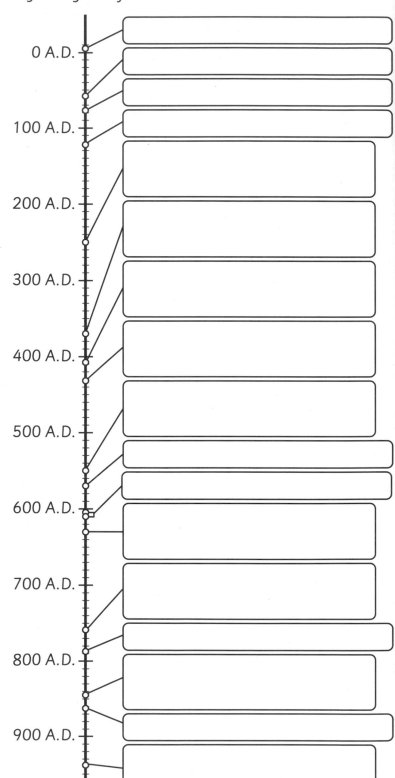

0 A.D.

100 A.D.

200 A.D.

300 A.D.

400 A.D.

500 A.D.

600 A.D.

700 A.D.

800 A.D.

900 A.D.

1000 A.D.

Name: Date:

Timeline: 0 to 1000

Our dating system begins with the year 0. Dates of years after this are known as 'A.D.' which is short for 'Anno Domini', meaning 'the year of our Lord'. Dates before the year 0 are known as B.C. which stands for 'Before Christ'. Historians now believe, however, that Jesus was probably born before the year 0, perhaps in the year 5 B.C.

Here is a list of some important events from the year 5 B.C. to the year 1000. They are not listed in order. Put them in order by neatly writing them in the appropriate places next to the time line.

844 A.D. - Kenneth MacAlpine becomes King of Scotland.

605 A.D. - 610 A.D. - Grand Canal built in China.

432 A.D. - St. Patrick takes Christianity to Ireland.

122 A.D. - Hadrian's Wall started.

757 A.D. - Offa builds Offa's Dyke between England and Wales.

250 A.D. - Roman Emperor orders persecution of Christians.

861 A.D. - Vikings discover Iceland.

370 A.D. - Europe invaded by Huns from Asia.

407 A.D. - Last Roman troops leave Britain.

58 A.D. - Buddhism introduced to China.

570 A.D. - Muhammad born in Mecca.

630 A.D. - Muhammad states the principles of Islam.

5 B.C. - Birth of Jesus

550 A.D. - St. David introduces Christianity to Wales.

981 A.D. - Eric the Red, a Viking, settles in Greenland.

77 A.D. - Romans conquer Britain.

937 A.D. - Athelstan claims to be King of Scotland.

787 A.D. - Britain attacked by Danes.

0 A.D.	Birth of Jesus.
	Buddhism introduced to China.
	Romans conquer Britain.
100 A.D.	Hadrian's Wall started.
	Roman Emperor orders persecution of Christians.
200 A.D.	Europe invaded by Huns from Asia.
300 A.D.	Last Roman troops leave Britain.
400 A.D.	St. Patrick takes Christianity to Ireland.
	St. David introduces Christianity to Wales.
500 A.D.	Muhammad born in Mecca.
	Grand Canal built in China.
600 A.D.	Muhammad states the principles of Islam.
700 A.D.	Offa builds Offa's Dyke between England and Wales.
	Britain attacked by Danes.
800 A.D.	Kenneth McAlpine becomes King of Scotland.
	Vikings discover Iceland.
900 A.D.	Athelstan claims to be King of Scotland.
1000 A.D.	Eric the Red, a Viking, settles in Greenland.

Name: Date:

Timeline: 1000 to 2000

Here is a list of some important events in British history over the last thousand years. The events are not listed in order. Put them in order by neatly writing them in the appropriate places next to the timeline…

<u>1642-1649</u>: English Civil War.

<u>1939-1945</u>: Second World War.

<u>1189</u>: Richard the Lionheart becomes King of England.

<u>1605</u>: Gunpowder Plot.

<u>1216</u>: Henry III becomes King of England at the age of 9.

<u>1653-1658</u>: Oliver Cromwell rules England.

<u>1776-1783</u>: War of American Independence from Britain.

<u>1666</u>: Great Fire of London.

<u>1588</u>: Spanish Armada defeated by English.

<u>1337</u>: The 'Hundred Years War' between England and France begins.

<u>1040-1057</u>: Macbeth is King of Scotland.

<u>1707</u>: England and Scotland become united.

<u>1837</u>: Victoria becomes Queen.

<u>1914-1918</u>: First World War.

<u>1306</u>: Robert the Bruce becomes King of Scotland.

<u>1400</u>: Owen Glendower proclaims himself Prince of Wales.

<u>1509</u>: Henry VIII becomes King of England.

<u>1542</u>: Mary Stuart becomes Queen of Scotland.

<u>1973</u>: Britain joins European Community.

<u>1558</u>: Elizabeth I becomes Queen of England.

<u>1807</u>: Slave Trade abolished in British Empire.

<u>1066</u>: Battle of Hastings, William the Conquerer invades England.

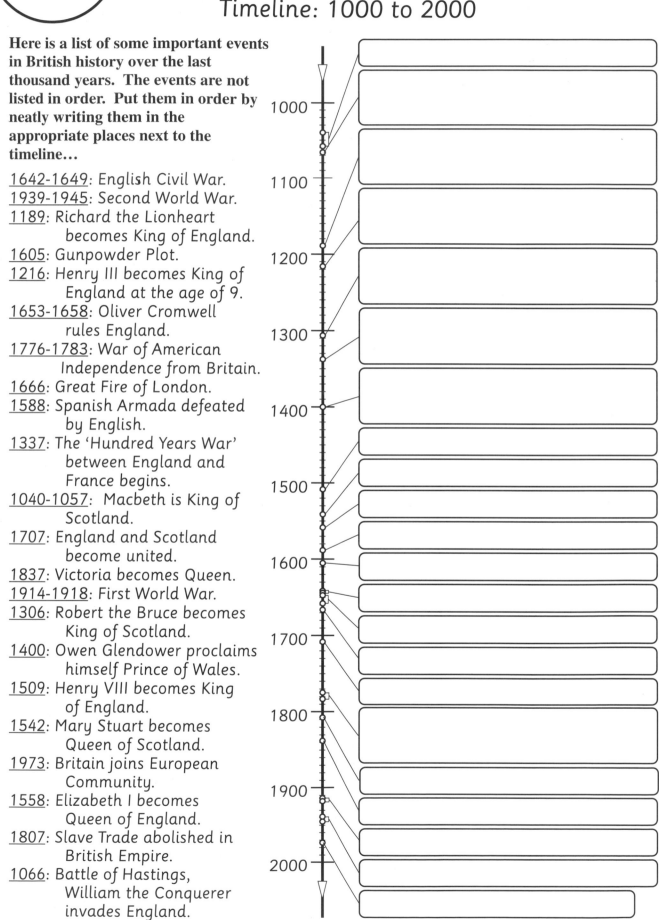

© Andrew Brodie *Publications* ✔ PO Box 23, Wellington, Somerset, TA21 8YX ✔ www.andrewbrodie.co.uk

Name: Date:

Timeline: 1000 to 2000

Here is a list of some important events in British history over the last thousand years. The events are not listed in order. Put them in order by neatly writing them in the appropriate places next to the timeline…

<u>1642-1649</u>: English Civil War.

<u>1939-1945</u>: Second World War.

<u>1189</u>: Richard the Lionheart becomes King of England.

<u>1605</u>: Gunpowder Plot.

<u>1216</u>: Henry III becomes King of England at the age of 9.

<u>1653-1658</u>: Oliver Cromwell rules England.

<u>1776-1783</u>: War of American Independence from Britain.

<u>1666</u>: Great Fire of London.

<u>1588</u>: Spanish Armada defeated by English.

<u>1337</u>: The 'Hundred Years War' between England and France begins.

<u>1040-1057</u>: Macbeth is King of Scotland.

<u>1707</u>: England and Scotland become united.

<u>1837</u>: Victoria becomes Queen.

<u>1914-1918</u>: First World War.

<u>1306</u>: Robert the Bruce becomes King of Scotland.

<u>1400</u>: Owen Glendower proclaims himself Prince of Wales.

<u>1509</u>: Henry VIII becomes King of England.

<u>1542</u>: Mary Stuart becomes Queen of Scotland.

<u>1973</u>: Britain joins European Community.

<u>1558</u>: Elizabeth I becomes Queen of England.

<u>1807</u>: Slave Trade abolished in British Empire.

<u>1066</u>: Battle of Hastings, William the Conquerer invades England.

Timeline markers: 1000, 1100, 1200, 1300, 1400, 1500, 1600, 1700, 1800, 1900, 2000

- Macbeth is King of Scotland.
- Battle of Hastings, William the Conqueror invades England.
- Richard the Lionheart becomes King of England.
- Henry III becomes King of England at age 9.
- Robert the Bruce becomes King of Scotland.
- The 'Hundred Years War' between England and France begins.
- Owen Glendower proclaims himself Prince of Wales.
- Henry VIII becomes King of England.
- Mary Stuart becomes Queen of Scotland.
- Elizabeth I becomes Queen of England.
- Spanish Armada defeated by English.
- Gunpowder plot.
- English Civil War.
- Oliver Cromwell rules England.
- Great Fire of London.
- England and Scotland become united.
- War of American Independence from Britain.
- Slave Trade abolished in British Empire.
- Victoria becomes Queen.
- First World War
- Second World War
- Britain joins European Community.

HOMEWORK TODAY *for ages 10 - 11*
Individual Record Sheet

Name:	Sheet	Date completed	Comment by parent / pupil / teacher.
Words and Numbers	1		
Multiplication Square	2		
Addition Grids	3		
Finding Change	4		
Measuring Angles	5		
Angles in a Triangle	6		
Magic Squares	7		
More Magic Squares	8		
Area and Perimeter	9		
More Area and Perimeter	10		
Sequences	11		
Adding Decimals	12		
Coordinates	13		
Handling Data 1	14		
Handling Data 2	15		
Handling Data 3	16		
The Moon	17		
Balloon Flight	18		
Verbs	19		
Nouns and Pronouns	20		
Adjectives	21		
Adverbs	22		
Singular and Plural	23		
Using Apostrophes 1	24		
Using Apostrophes 2	25		
Using Apostrophes 3	26		
Punctuation Practice 1	27		
Punctuation Practice 2	28		
Punctuation Practice 3	29		
Titanic	30		
Pairs of Words	31		
Morse Code	32		
Braille	33		
Odd Ones Out	34		
Cogs	35		
The Planets	36		
Earth and Sun	37		
Food Chains	38		
Plan of a School	39		
Using a Map	40		
Grid References	41		
Using the Scale	42		
Compass Directions	43		
The British Isles	44		
Some Towns and Cities	45		
Using the Scale	46		
United Kingdom: Points of reference	47		
Motorway routes	48		
Timeline: 0 to 1000	49		
Timeline: 1000 to 2000	50		